The Highland Estate Factor in the Age of the Clearances

Eric Richards

THE ISLANDS BOOK TRUST
Urras Leabhraichean nan Eilean
LIVING HISTORY

This lecture was given first to the Islands Book Trust in the County Hotel, Stornoway, on 26th August 2014. My warm thanks are due to the chairman, Alasdair MacEachen, and to John Randall who introduced me to so much of the geography, history and culture of the Long Island at that time. Another version was delivered as 'The Carnegie Lecture' to the University of the Highlands and Islands in Inverness on September 14th, 2014 and I wish to thank especially Dr David Worthington and his colleagues at the Centre for History in Dornoch for their great hospitality and assistance. The present text is an extended version of these lectures and I am extremely grateful to the Carnegie Trust of Scotland for funding the Centenary Professorship which made it all possible. I am also grateful to Dr Robert Fitzsimons and Dr Malcolm Bangor-Jones for their advice.

Eric Richards

Contents

I

The Carnegie Connection

A Lowlander of unmistakably humble origins, Andrew Carnegie in the 1890s was reputedly the richest man in the world.[1] He was also the most renowned and successful returned-migrant whose extraordinary philanthropy enriched libraries, educational bodies and peace movements across the Atlantic world. The Carnegie Trust is the living legacy of his munificence in Scotland. Carnegie finally chose to establish himself in the Highlands, recreating the life of the Highland laird at Skibo on the south-eastern corner of Sutherland. In the background as always, even at Skibo, was the estate manager, the Highland factor.

Andrew Carnegie, now the fabulously wealthy magnate of the United States steel industry, had travelled a long distance from his Scottish origins in Dunfermline. There was a curious parallel between his expatriation in the little Carnegie family to the United States in 1848, and the evacuations associated with a more contentious subject, namely the Highland Clearances.

---

1   David Nasaw, *Andrew Carnegie* (New York: Penguin Press, 2006), chap. 31, p. 586.

Carnegie's biographers, indeed Carnegie himself, regarded the Carnegie family as economic refugees, victims of technological change. William Carnegie, a master weaver of Dunfermline, had been ruined by the spread of the power looms into linen manufacture: the handloom weavers of Dunfermline were doomed. Technological change 'silenced the looms ... and the weavers were bereft'. The Carnegies had been 'reduced to poverty, the looms sold, the household effects auctioned for a pittance, and money was borrowed from relatives and a neighbour'. William, his wife Margaret and their two sons, Andrew and Thomas, followed the path of millions to the New World. As Jonathan Hughes says, 'their jobs disappeared under the forces of free trade and economic change ... There was nothing to do but leave Britain forever.' In this way Scotland and Europe 'lost part of its hardiest stock as a consequence, and America was the beneficiary.'[2]

Similar revolutionary forces were at work in the Highlands and Islands at this time. But here the expulsive forces were much more personalised and more directly attributable to the influence of the landlords, and even more directly to their employees, the estate factors in the Age of the Clearances. The factors played a central role in the story but they were not much admired nor, perhaps, understood.

---

2   Jonathan Hughes, *The Vital Few: American Economic Progress and Its Protagonists* (Boston: Houghton Mifflin, 1966), pp. 224-25. 'The Carnegie family had the misfortune to become one of economic history's great *causes célèbres*, the case of the handloom weavers, their impoverishment and destruction by the power loom.' Carnegie, despite his own family's story, eventually became an extremely influential advocate of technological change. He indeed celebrated the 'natural' elimination of the inefficient small producer, including the handloom weaver, and, no doubt, the crofter also. See Nasaw, *Andrew Carnegie*, p. 603.

II

The Reputation of the Factor

The reputation of the Highland factor, it need hardly be said, is seriously blemished. Leah Leneman, with masterly understatement, remarked that 'Praise for a factor was not a very common feature of Gaelic poetry.' Factors were the men who implemented the deeply unpopular policies which, in a shorthand, we call 'the Clearances'. But their reputation predates the Clearances: Robert Louis Stevenson, in *Kidnapped* (set after Culloden), depicts the factor as a figure of hatred, a man who met a nasty fate, who was indeed murdered.[3] Equally well known was a figure in lowland Ayrshire: Robert Burns's peasant family in Ayrshire lived in fear of the Steward, or Factor, whose letters and threatenings, Burns says, 'threw us all into tears'.[4] In

---

3   On the *Kidnapped* story see James Fergusson, 'The Appin Murder Case,' *Scottish Historical Review* 31 (1952), pp, 116-30. This was the murder of Colin Campbell of Glemure in 1752, Crown factor for the Ardshell estate, by a gunman. He was not, despite the romance, an oppressor of Jacobite tenants. See *Oxford Dictionary of National Biography*, vol. 52, pp. 628-29.

4   Thomas Carlyle, *On Heroes and Hero Worship* (1840), p. 250. See especially Burns' 'A New Lease' which features 'the factor's snash' and his stamping, threatening, cursing and swearing – quoted in Reay Clarke, *Two Hundred Years of Farming in Sutherland* (Kershader, South Lochs, Lewis: Islands Book Trust, 2014), p. 69.

Waverley, Walter Scott satirised such men of business as 'the Bailie MacWheebles of the time'. Modern historical novelists continue the tradition of revilement and satire.

Abominated, abused and castigated, the Highland factors' reputation is echoed down the decades. This demonology is well populated – and the worst offenders are well known even today, men who wielded great local authority over a dependent, poor and vulnerable crofter population. They used their position to harass, remove and oppress entire communities, decade after decade.

The most hated man in all modern Highland narratives is Patrick Sellar, sheep farmer and factor in Sutherland, charged with and exculpated of the crime of 'culpable homicide' in the removals of 1814. Sellar has been compared with Reinhard Heyrich who committed unspeakable atrocities against the Jews in Nazi-occupied Prague, an instrument of genocide.[5]

In Lewis the factor for Sir James Matheson for more than twenty years (1853-75), Donald Munro, was reviled even on his deathbed – his doctor allegedly asked for special antiseptics to cleanse away the contact he had had with the detested Munro.[6] The Lewis factor, who reigned over most of the population of the entire island, was regarded as a 'sneering, domineering tyrant' and 'irredeemably corrupt' – a man 'able to evict, exploit and oppress Matheson's thousands of crofting tenants'. He held down and humiliated a tenantry whom he treated with 'undisguised contempt'. He is depicted as a grotesque demon who typically 'combined

---

5   See Ian Grimble, in *Listener*, 5 March, 1964. More generally see Eric Richards, *Patrick Sellar and the Highland Clearances* (Edinburgh: Polygon at Edinburgh, 1999).

6   See the comprehensive denunciation of Munro by John MacLeod, '*None Dare Oppose': The Laird, the Beast and the People* (Edinburgh: Birlinn, 2010).

factorial power with multiple office-holding.'[7] Similarly, in Skye, Alexander MacDonald managed five estates, holding sway over 85% of the island population, and his name was still spoken with loathing as late as 1960. These were petty tyrants whose factorships were riddled with favouritism and nepotism.[8] When John Murdoch toured the Gordon estates in south Harris he was told that the people could not complain in case the factor 'would drive them from the estate'. Eviction was always the sharpest weapon in their armoury.

In Lewis, under Seaforth, the community lived under the power of the tacksmen as sub-factors (and ground officers in each parish), 'who looked on them as an inferior race and treated them accordingly'.[9] Under the Mathesons they were renowned for their acts of tyranny – the people were 'insulted, trampled upon and terrorised over.' The factors were described as raking off big profits from the kelp trade in its heyday.[10]

In the flood of testimonies before the Napier Commission in 1883 the factor at large was repeatedly castigated. Factors were said to have 'wielded the threat of eviction to exact

---

7   James Hunter, review of *'None Dare Oppose'*, by John MacLeod, *Northern Scotland* (May 2012), pp. 165-68. See also: Annie Tindley, '"They Sow the Wind, They Reap the Whirlwind": estate management in the post-clearance Highlands, c. 1815- c.1900', *Northern Scotland* 3 (2012), p.72. Antipathy towards factors was evident in the mid twentieth century: see R.H. Campbell, 'Valuations of Scottish Hill Sheep Stocks before 1941,' *Northern Scotland* 11 (1991), p. 62. See also Allan Campbell, 'The Freedom Legacy – A Personal View of the History of the Glendale Estate,' *Transactions of the Gaelic Society of Inverness*, LXVI (2010-2013) pp. 230 ff., which includes a three year old's witness in 1880 of the barbaric behaviour of the factor Norman MacRaild, as recollected almost nine decades later.

8   James Hunter, *The Making of a Crofting Community*, New edn. (Edinburgh: Birlinn, 2010), p. 176.

9   Donald Macdonald, *Lewis: A History of the Island* 2nd edn (Edinburgh: Wright, 1978), p.34.

10   John Munro Mackenzie, Chamberlain of the Lews, *Diary 1851* (Stornoway: Acair, 1994), p. 95.

obedience, [and] ruled as petty tyrants'. Typically Donald MacAskill in Dunvegan said, 'I am ashamed to confess it now that I trembled more before the factor than I did before the House of Lords.'[11] There was a long litany of complaint from all parts of the Highlands, often absolving the proprietors from blame. In Sutherland, the Reverend James Cumming, of Melness, the delegate elected by the people, reported that 'the agents of His Grace [the Duke of Sutherland] are his hands, his eyes, his ears and his feet, and in their dealings with people they are constantly like a wall of ice between his Grace and his Grace's people.'[12]

There is, of course, another side to this account. Leah Leneman, referring to the eighteenth-century estates of the Duke of Atholl, judged his factors as, on the whole, 'just men, and respected as such by the people of the estate.'[13] Sorley Maclean, speaking of the Gaelic poetic tradition, said there was 'an absurd tendency to blame the factor more than the landlord.'[14] The historian Allan Macinnes refers to these poetic traditions as the main outlet for public opinion, but 'usually expressed deferentially through misplaced strictures against factors, legal agents, tacksmen, incoming

---

11   I.M.M. Macphail, *The Crofters' War* (Stornoway, Lewis: Acair, 1989), p. 1.

12   *Napier Commission,* sitting at Bettyhill, Sutherland, 24 July 1883. Q. 25259. From the same district came a twentieth-century example of archaic attitudes among the authorities. This was recorded in the remarkable declaration of the Rhifail Estate factor in April 1924: writing of a recalcitrant crofter, he declared that he had 'never met Mackay [but] from what I hear he is a disturbing effect in Strathnaver. In several of his letters he said he was not a coward like some of his forebears who were burned out of Strathnaver, but it is a pity that the last dregs were not burned out at that same time.' Quoted in Iain J.M. Robertson, *Landscapes of Protest in the Scottish Highlands after 1914: The Later Highland Land Wars* (Farnham: Ashgate, 2013), p. 148.

13   Leah Leneman, *Living in Atholl: A Social History of the Estates* (Edinburgh: Edinburgh University Press, 1986), p. 66.

14   Quoted in Eric Richards, *Debating the Highland Clearances* (Edinburgh: Edinburgh University Press, 2007), p.82.

sheep farmers and even sheep'; recriminations against landlords were rare and usually generalised and entirely amorphous.[15] Joseph Mitchell in the 1860s was decidedly complimentary about the factors on the Seaforth estates. One of them operated as banker to the tenants, and was universally trusted and fair: he was 'reckoned throughout the district as secure as the Bank of England.' Mitchell characterised the factors on the Sutherland estates, including Evander MacIver in Scourie, as men of talent and integrity.[16]

The Highland estate factor undoubtedly controlled a great proportion of Highland life and welfare; on many estates they were delegated most of the landlord's authority, usually in the absence of the proprietor. They were, in effect, the local rulers. They were also the vital conductors of economic change. The factors were, of course, at the sharp end of the policy of evictions, clearances, resettlements and other radical changes in that age. They were invested with arbitrary authority and little local restraint apart from the slowly rising anger of the crofters at the end of the nineteenth century. They stood between the landlord and the tenantry, especially the small tenantry and they were expected to absorb criticism and often accepted the role of scapegoat.[17] They were the implementers, the enforcers, the 'doers', and eventually the modern managers.

15   I. Macinnes, 'Scottish Gaeldom: the First Phase of Clearance', in T. M. Devine and Rosalind Mitchison (eds), *People and Society in Scotland*, vol. 1 (Edinburgh: John Donald, 1988), p. 72.

16   Joseph Mitchell, *Reminiscences of My Life in the Highlands* (1883-84) vol. 2, pp. 47-48, 93. There were many variations among factors across the wide and differentiated experience of the Highlands; regional studies expose the full range of human diversity including many cases of compassionate factors who did their level best for the communities and landlords they served. Their histories are less well known, attracting less public expression in the annals of the north.

17   As Christina Byam Shaw remarks, 'some landlords used their factors as convenient buffers between themselves and their importunate crofter tenants', *Pigeon Holes of Memory*, 2nd edn (London: Constable, 1989), p. 279.

It was a profession which attracted many tough characters. None of them were actually murdered though some of them certainly faced threats to their lives. They were depicted as black-hearted Victorian figures, almost pantomime villains, but their status and their functions were real enough.

There is always a hazard in what the New Zealand novelist Lloyd Jones calls 'flash history' – where outrage and indignation take over from the ordinary and the commonplace. Beyond the accounts of individual factorial behaviour lies the question of why these men were in this position: that is, the context of factoring in the Highlands during the times of conflict and transformation. Their unsavoury reputation resided in the broad mesh of historical circumstances in the centre of which they were themselves entrapped.

III

The Age of the Managers

Land management in the Highlands had a long and contentious history. Scale was important. Landed estates, before the age of industrialisation, were usually the largest enterprises across the British Isles. This reflected the highly unequal distribution of wealth in pre-industrial society. Landed estates required elaborate systems of management and they were often based on longstanding practices which were slow to change. All of this applied as much to the Scottish Highlands as to the rest of the British Isles. It was never an easy task.

The emergence of a new class of managers was a prime requirement during early industrialisation.[18] Their long origins first emerged within the rural sector on the landed estates, mainly operated by a land-agent or chamberlain whose duties were diverse and often, especially in Scotland, closely connected with the legal profession. These people were the precursors of the modern manager, an 'executive' of one sort or another: powerful people, commonly charged

---

18   See Sidney Pollard, *The Genesis of Modern Management* (London: Arnold, 1968), p. 39

with re-shaping enterprises: reorganising, redeploying, moving resources and people around to achieve better 'outcomes'. Their work, in the modern world, has involved constant upsizing and downsizing and most often re-locating ordinary people.

The origins of this managerial class in the Highlands coincided with the period which witnessed the Clearances and their aftermath. It was time of accelerated change, restructuring the Highlands under new conditions, a new context. The old ways of running the Highland estate were challenged by new pressures – and the factor was at the centre of this long crisis in the Highlands.

The tasks of the Highland factor were more challenging than elsewhere partly because the profession developed more slowly while the pace of change descended upon them at an accelerated rate in the late eighteenth century. In the Highlands economic transformation was concertinaed – and this multiplied tensions for everyone, especially those charged with its execution.

Elsewhere the managerial changes pre-dated those in Scotland, north and south.

IV

The English Model

In England the 'improving steward' had already become a recognisable figure in the quickening changes in the rural scene by 1750, associated with the agrarian revolution. In their ranks emerged a cadre of 'men ... empowered to speak in the landlord's name, and ... charged with the duty of raising rents. They were bound to force the pace of agricultural change for this end, and poor tenants, lazy tenants or recalcitrant tenants now faced the threat of six months' notice, if they did not comply with the agent's directives.'[19] In England this level of direction was part of the assertion of greater control from the top, from the agent's office, which itself became increasingly professionalised.[20]

The way had long been paved. The erosion of small holdings in much of England and the creation of large capitalistic farms had already effectively eliminated the

---

19   See J.R. Wordie, 'Introduction' to C.W. Chalkin and J.R. Wordie (eds), *Town and Countryside* (London: Unwin Hyman, 1989), p. 18.

20   See for instance, Eric Richards, 'The Land Agent,' in G.E. Mingay (ed.), *The Victorian Countryside* 2 vols. (London: Routledge and Kegan Paul, 1981), Vol. 2, pp. 439-57.

peasant element which was overtaken by the emergence of the labourer class, a separate proletariat which became mainly the responsibility of the larger tenant farmers. The English land agent was therefore less intimately accountable for the direct management of the mass of the rural population. Rural England was being converted into the familiar three-tier system (landlords, tenant farmers, labourers).

In England the small occupier was largely eliminated much earlier than elsewhere in the British Isles. Estate administration was thereby streamlined towards a tenantry of substantial farmers who dealt with their workforce directly, even to the point of displacing family farming, especially in the south and east of England, even by 1700. The earlier consolidation of land and enclosure in England in the previous decades had generated a powerful language of condemnation: in vehemence this record of rural protest matched that of other parts of the British Isles as they passed through a not dissimilar process in later centuries.[21]

These changes can be traced from the seventeenth century but clearly emerged most significantly by 1750;[22] they were associated with greater absenteeism by the landlord class, meanwhile management became 'more thorough and scientific' as the production of the landed estates became more complex with widening economic activities.[23] Before 1750 estates were generally managed by the gentry

---

21   A few samples of contemporary English emotion and anger are displayed in, for instance, R. E. Prothero, Lord Ernle, *English Farming: Past and Present*, 6th edn (London: Heinemann, 1961), p. 60-65.

22   See Janie Cottis, 'A Country Gentleman and his Estates,' in C.W. Chalkin and J.R. Wordie (eds), *Town and Countryside* (London: Unwin Hyman, 1989), p. 27; and P.J. Keeley, 'A Devon family and their estates,' in Chalkin, *Town and Countryside*, p. 189.

23   See David Oldroyd, *Estates, Enterprise and Investment at the Dawn of the Industrial Revolution* (Aldershot: Ashgate, 2007), pp. 23-24, 25-27.

themselves. This was a transition later replicated in the Highlands.[24]

One of the key elements in the managerial changes in England was the imposition of a much greater degree of control over the tenantry by means shorter leases, and more positive and specific instructions regarding farming practices – all reinforced by skilled dedicated professional estate officials.[25] The management framework was made more directive and 'Improvement'-oriented, and became the widely-recommended model.

There were other key shifts in rural life which amounted to the assertion of greater landlord control and systematisation in rural management. One was the removal of long leases, which allowed much more immediate control over rents, investment and agricultural practices. The consolidation of this system also made farmers more directly responsive to landlord directives and market opportunities. The erosion of small holdings and the creation of large capitalistic farms was a central evolution, much enhanced by the execution of enclosures which further weakened the place of the small holder on the land. The English system of agriculture was simplified, notably with the effective elimination of the peasant element, overtaken by the

---

24 One of the main changes in English estate management was to take it out of the hands of family connections; the separation is chronicled by D.R. Hainsworth, in *Stewards, Lords and People* (Cambridge: Cambridge University Press, 1992).

25 See David Spring, *The English Landed Estate in the Nineteenth Century* (Baltimore: Johns Hopkins, 1963), pp. 55-134; Wordie, *Town and Countryside,* pp. 18, 53-4, 214-15. The management of English estates is essayed by J.V. Beckett, *The Aristocracy in England, 1660-1914* (Oxford: Blackwell, 1986), pp.139-49; scattered estates required a degree of coordination. Shortages of good people led to higher salaries – as high as £1800 for the Duke of Bedford in 1861: see, Beckett, *Aristocracy*, p. 144. Absenteeism was a general problem: in 1871 sixty individuals controlled two-thirds of England. Peculation was rife and stories of corrupt stewards legion: see Beckett, p. 154.

emergence of the labourer class, a separate proletariat which was mainly the responsibility of the farmers whose own scale had increased in the midst of these changes. Large-scale agrarian capitalists were replacing family farmers: they now employed a paid labour force – so that proletarianised agriculture became the prevailing model for the future.[26]

A loud mantra echoed across England – it declared that 'Improvement' essentially depended 'on the existence of compact, consolidated farm units.'[27] Modernisation in England was probably implemented more easily because the small occupiers had to a much greater degree already been eliminated. Estate management was more streamlined towards dealing with large tenants on a strictly commercialised basis. In the Highlands and in Ireland the transition had not proceeded nearly so far; consequently the roles of the tacksman and of the factor were more onerous. On top of this Highland landlords began to nurture ambitions of new enterprise: to build villages, so keeping up with the Lowland Joneses. Management became more complicated.

In England, therefore, the great changes in the management of rural productivity were accomplished more easily than elsewhere, mainly because the system had already been prepared. In some ways the English land agent's responsibilities became more onerous and technical, responsible for the onward revolution in rural productivity; but simultaneously their work was simplified – they were not intimately accountable for the direct management of the mass of the rural population.

It is also clear that even in England there existed a continuing tension in the marked shift towards the pursuit

---

26   See Leigh Shaw Taylor, in 'The rise of agrarian capitalism and the decline of family farming in England', *Economic History Review,* vol. 65 (2012), pp. 26-60.

27   Beckett, *Aristocracy*, pp 26-7.

of profit while the same landlords hoped to 'still remain feudal in orientation'.[28] These were complicated evolutions even in the most capitalistic rural society and many generations passed before their full maturation and acceptance. Even as late as 1800 the fully professional 'land agents' remained a minority, especially where estates were still tied up with three-lives leases (in which system the old attorney figure also persisted).[29] 'The old idea that an estate was a unit of consumption rather than of management was slowly dying out.' The agent had to be 'alert and knowledgeable', the driving force for improvement.[30]

The conversion to large farms in England required the ousting of smaller farmers, 'getting rid of the wrong ones'. The work of weeding out old tenantry continued and in 1849 Sir Charles West predicted that 'small unskilful farmers [would] share the fate of the handloom weavers'.[31] (This was a clear echo of the Carnegies' experience in Dunfermline.) It also required the ending of the old convention of hereditary tenancies, which was far from popular. Under modern management there was a much closer supervision of tenants under leases – and rendered highly market oriented. Agents were also heavily involved in local government – in the Poor Law, as JPs, social conservatives enforcing law and order and general morality. This was the model adopted very widely; but it was more difficult in other parts of the British

---

28   Ibid., p. 25.

29   See J.A. Chartres, 'Country trades, crafts and professions,' in *The Agrarian History of England and Wales*, vol. 6: 1750-1850, edited by G. E. Mingay (London: Cambridge University Press, 1989), p. 451. Part of the change was in name – 'agents' instead of 'stewards' – which was part of the growing professional self-consciousness.

30   See J.V. Beckett, in Mingay (ed.), *Agrarian History*, vol. 6, p.590. Talent was in short supply and big salaries were paid to the top managers; see Spring, *English Landed Estate*, p. 93. The pay scales of Highland factors are considered in Tindley, 'They sow', p.70.

31   Spring, *English Landed Estate*, p. 111.

Isles. And even in England there were serious tensions, even outright conflict, in the marked shift towards the more systematic pursuit of profit.[32] These changes were associated with greater degrees of absenteeism by the landlord class.[33]

In England there was a recurring paradox: many landlords wanted to retain their old social status and role, to 'remain feudal in orientation'.[34] In effect the landlord often harboured notions of *noblesse oblige*, of the old paternalism. Consequently 'strictly commercial grounds' were not easily assimilated into this psychology. The increasing contradiction between tradition and modernity made life difficult for the land agent who was commonly under the new orders and priorities. And as the English land agent became more powerful and vital, and indeed more highly salaried and professional, so the social distance between landlord and tenant seemed to widen.[35] Thus 'Agents were primarily concerned with maximising efficiency and income, but the owner needed to draw a

---

32   The extent of opposition to rural restructuring is not always clear: e.g. anti- enclosure actions – but see Janet Neeson, *Commoners: Common Right, Enclosure and Social Change in Common-Field England, 1700-1820* (Cambridge: Cambridge University Press, 1993), chapter 9; Neeson talks about the 'deep hostility generated by enclosure' which was 'corrosive of social relations'; see also David Eastwood, *Governing Rural England* (Oxford: Clarendon Press, 1985), pp. 237-38, which records anti -enclosure riots as late as 1830-35 in Otmoor, Oxfordshire.

33   See Oldroyd, *Estates, Enterprise*, pp. 23-24, 25-27.

34   Ibid., p. 25.

35   In some parts the remnants of the old order persisted longer: small estates continued to be run by manorial stewards or by the owner him or herself, or by second-class gentlemen, or less well-off relatives, or lesser gentry figures (parallels with the tacksmen spring to mind). And throughout these changes there remained a common 'propensity of tenants to appeal to the owner over the head of the agent'. It was evidently an invidious position, even in England. See J.A. Chartres, 'Country Trades', p. 451. There was a tension between the commercial aspirations of the owners and their advisors and their perceptions of their traditional roles in rural society. See J.V. Beckett, 'Land ownership and estate management,' in Mingay (ed.), *Agrarian History*, p.590.

fine distinction between his economic return and his socio-political interest'.[36]

There was considerable resentment against the rise and influence of estate agents, even in England. Thus in 1815 a Salopian farmer complained that 'Formerly the tenant had access to and could communicate his own griefs to his own landlord, and was heard patiently, but now forsooth, if we have anything to complain of, we are told the agent must hear and determine.'[37] On the Sutherland estates, in the Highlands and in Midland England, the tenantry were not given direct access to the noble family; in the first instance they addressed the agents and factors and were usually blocked from taking the matter further.[38]

By 1750 most estate management in England was already passing from the gentry and their kinfolk to their agents, a pattern later replicated, with important variations, in Lowland Scotland and in the Scottish Highlands. Eventually the land agency business in England recruited talent from across the country but disproportionately from Scotland, especially drawing upon the legal profession and the Scottish apprenticeship system in agency offices, and articled surveyors.[39] Scots thus became prominent in the control of English estates; they were models of probity, acting as

36   Beckett, 'Land ownership,' p. 597.

37   *Shrewsbury Chronicle,* 13 July 1815.Cf the discussion of English land agents in Carol Beardmore,' Landowner, Tenant and Agent on the Marquis of Anglesey's Dorset and Somerset Estate, 1814-46,' *Rural History,* 26 (20150, pp. 182-5.

38   When the Duke of Sutherland or any of the family visited the estates they were closely monitored and protected by the resident agents and factors. It was the accepted protocol in Sutherland and when breached caused great umbrage.

39   See J.H. Porter, 'The development of rural society,' in Mingay (ed.), *Agrarian History,* p. 844. On Scots in England, see Spring, *English Landed Estate,* pp. 86, 99; and also J.D. Chambers and G.E. Mingay, *The Agricultural Revolution 1750-1880* (London: Batsford, 1966), p.184. On the training and recruitment of Highland factors, see Tindley, 'They sow', p.69.

lightning rods of change and attitudes. Their influence extended much further in the Empire: many Scots were conspicuous as managerial figures in India, Australia and, most of all, in the slave plantations of the Caribbean.[40]

40   There has been a considerable circulation and interchange of factors within and beyond the Highlands. Scotland was a provider of rural management personnel across the world, indeed as far as Australia. Scots, including Highlanders, were particularly prominent in the management of slave plantations, see B.W. Higman, *Plantation Jamaica, 1750-1850* (Kingston: University of Jamaica Press, 2005), passim. The spread of 'Enlightenment' ideas about 'scientific' management in the slave plantations offers a parallel to developments in the Highlands. See, for instance, the remarks of Benjamin Sacks, in *Reviews in History*, no 1584 (2014).

V

The League Table of Reputations: Wales, Ireland and the Highlands

The role of the land agent varied according to the needs and imperatives of rural circumstances and the range across the British Isles was extreme. In eighteenth-century rural Wales, for instance, population growth and structural changes in the foundations of land use were generally more fundamental than in England; alternative employment for displaced people was generally less available. According to a Welsh historian, Geraint Jenkins, by the late eighteenth century 'many landed estates had fallen into the hands of landlords who, if they were not already English, simply adopted metropolitan values and distanced themselves from the native culture and the tongue spoken by the vast majority.' Jenkins talks of the growing social distance 'especially as hard-hearted stewards and agents violated the traditional code of conduct which had previously bound the social groups together.' He quotes William Jones of the Wynnstay Estate in Montgomeryshire, referring to agents as 'these rapacious cormorants'.[41] This was a recipe for conflict and Wales was witness to some classic rifts in the rural fabric.[42] There were evident echoes of the Highlands in the Welsh experience.

There was no such unclarity about the reputation of the agent in Ireland and there are strong parallels with the unhappy experience of the Highlands. But conflict in rural Ireland was vastly greater and proportional to the more catastrophic conditions that burdened that country.[43] Landed estate management in Ireland had to cope with the over-whelming problem of population pressure, congestion and subsistence crises and ultimately with the Great Famine of the 1840s.[44] In much of Ireland the rural managers were

41   Geraint H. Jenkins, *A Concise History of Wales* (Cambridge: Cambridge University Press, 2007), p. 191-92.

42   See David W. Howell, *Land and People in Nineteenth-Century Wales* (London: Routledge, 1977), pp. 620-3 where he provides a detailed view of Welsh land agencies, suggesting that a minority of them were unprincipled and unscrupulous (pp. 42-46). There is clear evidence of resistance to change in rural Wales – to rent rises, to land hunger, to the shortening leases, to enclosures and the removal of squatters, the loss of commons, and consolidation, especially from the 1790s. Some of this obloquy was turned against the agents. See David J. V. Jones, *Before Rebecca: Popular Protest in Wales 1793-1835* (London: Allen Lane, 1973), pp. 35-45. A recurring theme was the tenacious attachment to the family farm, the assault on which, by evictions, produced the greatest opposition, often reinforced by religious elements – once more suggesting direct similarities with the Highlands .

43   The Irish case was captured by J.C. Beckett as it related to the competition for the land and how it should be used. This was the nerve centre of rural relations: 'What concerned the tenant most was security – an assurance that his lease, when it fell in, would be renewed on terms that he could accept. Nothing created so much bitterness as an attempt by the landlord or his agent to turn a tenant out of his holding.' *Aspects of Irish Social History, 1750-1800* (Northern Ireland: Public Record Office, 1969), p.xi.

44   The tensions, of course, pre-dated the Famine. In 1835, the Scottish traveller Robert Graham, of Redgarton, observed in southern Ireland that 'the very respectable man who fills the quiet occupation of a shepherd never stirs an inch without a pair of pistols in his pocket.' He also noted that the agent's residence was strengthened in its defences, exactly 'like a garrison'. Henry Heaney (ed.), *A Scottish Whig in Ireland, 1835-38* (Dublin: Four Courts,

required to conduct vast structural changes compared with which events in the rest of the British Isles pale into relative insignificance. In a nutshell, a great many Irish estates followed policies of population reduction, of eviction, of induced emigration, and the elimination of small holders. The eventual outcome was the conversion of much of the rural population into a proletariat. The fiercest execution of the policy occurred at the time of the Famine: between 1849 and 1853 some 45,000 families were evicted in Ireland.[45] By the mid-1850s the numbers were much reduced – to about 1000 per annum and mass eviction became rarer. Nevertheless the demission of the peasantry proceeded decade by decade.

Inevitably the Irish estate agent was the primary implementer of these changes and he became a hated figure across the countryside.[46] The exercise of landlord power inflamed popular anger,[47] as in County Monaghan where in

---

1999), p. 100. James A. Donnelly notes the rising status of land agents in Ireland in the nineteenth century in *Land and People of Nineteenth-Century Cork* (London: Routledge, 1975), chapter IV. On eighteenth-century northern Irish estate agents and their heightened duties, see Rosemary Richey, 'The Eighteenth-Century Estate Agent and his Correspondence: County Down: A Case Study', in R.J. Morris and Liam Kennedy (eds), *Ireland and Scotland: Order and Disorder, 1600-2000* (Edinburgh: John Donald, 2005), especially pp. 43-44.

45   W. E. Vaughan, *Landlords and Tenants in Ireland, 1848-1904* (Economic and Social History Society of Ireland, 1984), p.23. There are estimates of 90,000 evictions between 1847 and 1890; 50,000 of these between 1847 and 1850. The connection between clearances, poverty and violence on Irish estates is further exposed in Ciarán J. Reilly, 'Clearing the Estates to Fill the Workhouse: King's County Land Agents and the Irish Poor Law act of 1838', in Virginia Crossman and Peter Gray (eds) *Poverty and Welfare in Ireland 1838-1948* (Dublin: Irish Academic Press, 2011).

46   The most infamous case of all was that of Captain Boycott, an English-born ex-soldier agent for Lord Erne's Co. Mayo estate in the years after 1873. He served eviction notices to tenants in arrears leading to a veritable cascade of consequences and the famous ostracisation in a highly charged political context which led eventually to the intervention of troops in 1880. See Joyce Marlow, *Captain Boycott and the Irish* (London: Deutsch, 1973).

47   The general reputation was famously epitomised by the oft-quoted

1843 great bonfires were lit across the Shirley estates to celebrate the death of the agent, Sandy Mitchell.[48]

In Ireland the peasantry's reaction to mass evictions and changes to the land systems produced widespread violence amounting to 'sporadic guerrilla activity' among the 'traditionally minded, entrenched peasantry'. Michael Beames has provided a detailed analysis of the assassination victims in the decades before the Great Famine, pinpointing the factors and landlords as targets, especially in Tipperary.[49] Similarly in King's County between 1830 and 1852 four landlords, seven agents and four estate employees were murdered, and many more than twenty others shot or injured. A contemporary report talked of the plight of land agents who suffered festering wounds, fractured skulls, broken limbs, and bodies perforated with bullets or shot, their assailants often egged on by the priests. In Ireland between 1857 and 1878 nine landlords, one agent, seven bailiffs and ten other servants were murdered.[50] It was not surprising.[51]

---

report from Great Blasket Island where 'the landlords were sometimes decent men, they will tell you, but the agents were devils one and all'. See Robin Flower, *The Western Island or the Great Blasket* (New York: Oxford University Press, 1945), p. 37.

48   Ciáran Reilly, *The Irish Land Agent, 1830-60* (Dublin: Four Courts, 2014), p. 53.

49   See Michael Beames, *Peasants and Power* (Sussex: Harvester Press, 1983), the appendices; and M.R. Beames, 'Rural Conflict in Pre-Famine Ireland: Peasant Assassinations in Tipperary, 1837-1847', in C.H.E. Philpin (ed.), *Nationalism and Popular Protest in Ireland* (Cambridge: Cambridge University Press, 1987).

50   But Vaughan notes that seven of these homicides were 'accounted for by only three incidents'. Vaughan surprisingly says that in proportional terms this was not great and that it was more dangerous to be an English gamekeeper than an Irish bailiff. But landlords were at more risk. See W.E. Vaughan, *Sin, Sheep and Scotsmen: John George Adair and the Derryveagh Evictions, 1861* (Belfast, 1983), p. 34. In his *Murder Trials in Ireland, 1836-1914* (Dublin: Four Courts Press, 2009, p. 58), Vaughan refers to the category 'agrarian assassinations', but suggests they were a relatively small fraction of ordinary homicides.

51   The detestation of the land agent in Ireland is documented in W.A.

28

In Ireland, according to W. E. Vaughan, the agent always had the discretionary authority and power to evict a tenant, which 'kept the people in a state of constant apprehension.'[52] Irish land agents (sometimes called 'factors') consequently attained an unrivalled reputation – 'a black catalogue of dishonesty, oppression and treachery', though this characterisation has been somewhat modified by modern scholarship.[53] Scots were notably involved in the Irish turmoil. Thus at Derryveagh in County Donegal in the early 1860s, the landowner, George Adair, cleared 244 people and unroofed or levelled twenty-eight houses in order to introduce Scots sheep and Scots shepherds. The Scots were deeply unpopular as was their Scottish land steward, James Murray.[54]

In Donegal this process had created turmoil on several estates, leading to widespread sheep thefts and killings. Murray himself was murdered and the agents generally loathed and the crisis was followed by further mass evictions and parliamentary enquiries. The public outrage was a clear echo of Highland indignation which was building in the same decades: in Donegal the landlords and their agents were denounced for the 'driving out of the native Gaelic-speaking population from their ancestral land, where they had dwelt for "twice a thousand years," and their replacement by Scots sheep.'[55] This profound transition precipitated mounting agitation. In the popular mind the spread of pastoral farming was the ultimate cause of 'the extinction

---

Maguire, *The Downshire Estates in Ireland, 1801-1845* (Oxford: Clarendon Press, 1972), chap vi, pp.183-84. The agents were often depicted as the heartless oppressors of the tenantry.

52   W.E. Vaughan, *Landlords and Tenants in Mid-Victorian Ireland* (Oxford, 1994), pp. 103-4.

53   See Reilly, *Irish Land Agent*, p. 13.

54   This entailed the eviction of forty-seven families in 1861; the Scottish steward was murdered.

55   Vaughan, *Sin, Sheep*, p. 23.

of the Irish race by enforced emigration.' Indeed many of the evictees fled to Queensland. The Scots were their *bêtes noires*.[56]

In accounting the reputation of the Highland estate factor it is therefore useful to bear in mind the parallel lives of their counterparts in the rest of the British Isles. For it was a common claim that that while in Ireland the agent was shot, the Highlanders were generally more placid. Indeed in the league table of popular detestation, Irish land agents were the most hated; the least reviled were the English and those of Wales, with the Highland estate factors located somewhere between.

A common theme in these passages of rural turmoil in different places across Britain was of land agents cast as the instruments of structural change. The reputation of the Highland estate factor accurately registered the work they were required to undertake. But the reputation of Highland factors tends to be associated with particular individuals, their personal attributes, personalities and attitudes. Yet their reputation at large was subject to another pattern which is identifiable across the British Isles, in these comparative historical stakes. Within the Highlands and Islands the factors were most unpopular in the furthest edges of the region: their reputation, in general, was most severe and despised in the furthest north and west of the region, and there were specific reasons why this was so.

---

56   See Vaughan, *Sin, Sheep*, pp. 17, 20, 22, 23, 29, 34. Irish evictions in the late nineteenth century brought in large-scale graziers of many sorts, including land agents, bailiffs and former middlemen: 'creatures of the rent office,' as they were termed. In the west of Ireland much of the cleared land, mainly upland pasture, 'was given to Scottish and northern English sheep farmers'. See David S. Jones, 'The Cleavage between Graziers and Peasants in the Land Struggle, 1890-1910', in Samuel Clark and James S. Donnelly Jnr. (ed.), *Irish Peasants: Violence and Political Unrest, 1780-1914* (Manchester: Manchester University Press, 1983), pp. 394-95.

VI

The Scottish and Highland Systems

In Scotland in general, the old estate administration system persisted longer and became more professionalised somewhat later. The role of factor and chamberlain was often intermixed and undertaken by well-to-do tenants or, in the north, by lesser relatives of the landlord and especially by tacksmen who retained much local autonomy in their control of large parts of estate administration.[57] The tacksmen usually performed factoring roles until the system became professionalised and then social distances widened. It echoed the English story.[58]

---

57   The tacksmen had generally managed the subtenantry and they formed a crucial middle stratum, answerable to the landlords from whom they received leases or tacks over wide stretches of Highland estates. They sublet to the small tenants and naturally skimmed off any surplus they could extract. They wielded much authority, sometimes to the point of extreme severity, though this depended on personality and circumstances. By the 1770s they were widely involved as brokers for emigration agents across the Highlands.

58   Malcolm Bangor-Jones, 'Settlement, society and field systems in the improvement era,' in *Scottish Life and Society*, vol. 2: *Farming and the Land*, edited by Alexander Fenton and Kenneth Veitch (Edinburgh: John Donald in association with the European Ethnological Research Centre, 2011), p. 135.

An English observer of mid-eighteenth century Scotland remarked:

> there is hardly such a thing as what they call in England a land steward regularly bred to that service; what is called a factor here seems to be only a sort of agent and receiver, which is a mightly small part indeed of an English land steward's business.

In England the estate agent was crucially responsible to impose extensive measures of 'Improvement' across the agricultural scene. This function was slower to emerge in Scotland.[59] Yet Scottish agriculture undoubtedly accelerated into 'Improvement' and within a few decades Scotland became a world leader in agricultural practice and rural restructuring.

Eventually a new class of Scottish estate factors emerged, some of them university-trained, who became crucial conduits of ideas and practice with new tiers of estate administration. Factors had to tread carefully – so that tenants could reap a reasonable return under fair and equitable rents – to encourage efficiency and agricultural progress. Across the Lowlands the broad process of transformation was at work, usually involving the creation of larger units and the eradication of subletting.[60] The estate factors were the instruments of improvement, mainly after 1760 when demand for output in agriculture began to exceed supply – and this generated a positive response on the supply side.[61]

In the Highlands, after Culloden, conditions were exceptional and the model of agrarian change highly

59   See Ian Whyte, 'The agents of Agricultural change', in M.L. Parry and T.R. Slater (eds), *The Making of the Scottish Countryside* (London: Croom Helm, 1980), pp. 165ff.

60   See T.M. Devine, *Clearance and Improvement: Land, Power and People in Scotland 1700-1900* (Edinburgh: John Donald, 2006), p. 53

61   See T.C. Smout, 'A New Look at the Scottish Improvers', *Scottish Historical Review* 91 (2012), pp. 125-49.

unusual. Here, in many parts of the subjugated post-1746 Highlands, the transformation was imposed from above by the Commissioners of the Annexed and Forfeited Estates. The Commissioners were, in effect, central planners charged with the responsibility not only to administer the Forfeited Estates but also to transform the very foundations of economic and social life across the Highlands. They delegated their authority to managers or factors. Under the central scrutiny of the Annexed Estates Board the factors were strictly forbidden to accept presents from tenants, a common temptation. Salaries were usually calculated on 5% of the rents which varied in line with grain prices. Part of their function was to show 'great zeal and activity in civilising the Highlands.'[62] In 1778 'this early experiment of government intervention in regional development came to an end.'[63] Nevertheless the administration by the Board had left its mark on the Highlands and its work was imitated and replicated by many Highland landlords whose local power and concentrated ownership allowed them to reorganise the economic and social life in the north.

Even before Culloden, and before the work of the Commissioners, several landlords were already reorganising their estates, responding as always to shifting market opportunities. The structures of management were therefore pressed to implement the new estate requirements. For instance, major changes were being implemented on the Argyll Estates as early as the 1730s; a much more

---

62   The factors employed by the Commissioners of the Jacobite Estates were specifically required to institute changes; but they were also required to perform paternalistic functions, especially meal supply and distribution of relief in times of scarcity, as well as education and innovation. See Annette M. Smith, 'The Forfeited Annexed Estates 1752-1784', in *The Scottish Tradition*, edited by G.W.S. Barrow (Edinburgh: Scottish Academic Press, 1974), pp. 36-49, 52.

63   Smith, 'Forfeited annexed estates', p. 209.

professional approach on the Atholl Estates had been introduced by 1741, particularly characterised by the manip- ulation of leases, which became a vital tool of legal agents who guided the management.[64] Generally, however, agrarian reorganisation took much longer than in the Lowlands. Lawyers often managed the finances of landowners from a distance, not always giving total satisfaction. As late as 1809, Elizabeth Grant of Rothiemurchus reported on the profession from a visit to Inverness:

> None of the Lairds of our north Countrie managed their own affairs, all were in the hands of some little writer body who to judge the consequences ruined most of their clients. One of these leeches generally sufficed for ordinary victims. My dear father was preyed on by two or three, of which honourable fraternity Arthur Cooper was the most distinguished for iniquity.[65]

Adam Smith himself was sceptical of the value of such agents.

In terms of Improvement many parts of the Highlands were playing catch-up, not unlike the situation in much of Ireland. Often the result, when it came, forced change at an accelerated pace compared with the relative gradualism of the Lowlands.[66] It was a recipe for heightened tension and opposition within the affected communities.

Although the professionalisation of estate administrations eventually extended across the entire country, the problems of estate management in the Highlands were of a different order: the scale and intensity, and the challenge were magnified

---

64   Leneman, *Living in Atholl*, p. 28

65   Elizabeth Grant, *Memoirs of a Highland Lady,* I (London: John Murray, 1928), pp. 116-17.

66   See R.A. Dodgshon, in Elizabeth Foyster and Christopher A. Whatley (eds), *A History of Everyday Life in Scotland 1600 to 1800* (Edinburgh: Edinburgh University Press, 2010), p. 35.

by the special circumstances in the Highlands in these decades. Part of the function of the new cadre in Highland management was to systematise the old customary occupation of the land and introduce regular leasing and rental arrangements, again generating resentments and opposition. It was a long struggle to impose new order on a remote zone.[67]

By the end of the eighteenth century many factors were required by their masters to operate the apparatus of removal and resettlement, and this involved the direction of the teams doing the actual evicting or re-locating. Implementing these changes, in the first instance, rested on the shoulders of the old managerial class – the chamberlains, the small landholders, the tacksmen. They became increasingly vital in conducting the transformation – and eventually this *corps* tended to attract the lion's share of the opprobrium which inevitably accompanied the changes. They were at the sharp end of the transformation of the region. Allegations of individual acts of savagery, inhumanity and criminal behaviour, tarnished the entire profession. Much of this was self-incrimination, confirmed from their own documentation preserved so professionally in factors' estate records. But most often their own record was couched in terms of pride and moral confidence: there was never a hint of contrition, rather a litany of self-justification.

The role of the factor was described by the Agricultural Reporter, Henderson, speaking of the Sutherland Estates at the time of the first clearances. Their duties, he remarked, went far beyond the mere collection of rents: 'with the proprietors' consent, [the factor] grants leases and removes tenants, he holds Baron-Baillie Courts to settle petty disputes between the tenantry, acts as Vice-Lieutenant of the County, and is a leading man in all county meetings.'

---

67   See Rab Houston, 'Custom in Context: Medieval and Early Modern Scotland and England', *Past and Present*, no. 211 (2011), esp. pp. 56-59.

R.J. Adam likened the factor to a 'great mediaeval lord's bailiff'.[68]

The method of recruiting Highland factors was varied, and many of them moved between estates over their careers. Their numbers included some dynasties of factors, who ruled certain estates over many decades – such as the Lochs, the Shaws and the Gillanders. Some were apprenticed in factors' offices, some were brought in from adjacent estates or from a distance; others were attracted from the south of Scotland and the Islands, with or without knowledge of Gaelic. Some were educated and well lettered, others on small estates were barely literate or numerate. There was no clear pattern except that of rising professionalisation and rising salaries. Some were very well paid and aspired to an elevated social status of their own. There was a greater turnover of factors in the late eighteenth and early nineteenth centuries. The fact that many factors became proprietors in their own right suggests their success in the profession. Rivalries also operated, one factor displacing another. In Sutherland in the first decade of the new century, the factor Cosmo Falconer had unseated his own predecessor, but Falconer himself was subsequently removed under the influence of Patrick Sellar. Sellar denounced Falconer to his employers as fat, lazy and incompetent: this was part of his systematic subversion of Falconer who was eventually ousted and replaced by Sellar himself. Falconer, like Sellar, had been trained in the estate office of Sellar's father in Elgin.[69] Sellar's own career as factor was suddenly terminated when he faced the charge of culpable homicide: he subsequently concentrated his ample energies on sheep farming.

---

68   R.J. Adam (ed.), *John Home's Survey of Assynt* (Edinburgh: Constable, for the Scottish History Society, 1960), p. 67.

69   See Eric Richards, *Patrick Sellar*, pp. 53-61, 63-66, 71-73, 87, 125.

VII

Special Conditions in the Highland Crisis

The scale of the challenge in the Highlands was magnified by the special circumstances in these decades. The Highland estate factors faced unprecedented demands which inevitably placed them in the middle of severe controversies and, most of all, at the centre of the Highland Crisis in the decades from 1780 to 1850. The crisis had several dimensions; some it determined externally, some generated from within. Eventually the Highland factor, as we have already noted, became the central figure in the demonology of the Clearances, feared and reviled across the region over many decades, accounted responsible for the turmoil and anger of the times.

The Highland factor began to emerge as a small but now specialised and professional cadre by the end of the eighteenth century, often displacing the previous widespread dependence on the tacksman class upon whom much of the old estate management had been traditionally devolved.[70]

---

70   In the pre-clearance world the tacksmen had often incurred an unsavoury reputation. Dodgshon remarks that 'as soon as the documentary

This takeover was itself a source of intense and continuing conflict in Highland communities. Moreover, the estate factor's responsibilities grew as the estates were increasingly drawn into deeper commercial entanglements with the rest of the British and Atlantic economies. Highland estates became differently used, and more diversified in their production and marketing. To the old cattle trade was added kelp and fishing and, most decisively and disruptively, sheep farming. Added to these changes were the development of villages and the normal subsistence requirements of the estates.

Simultaneously the estates were faced with totally unprecedented demographic conditions, numbers doubling and more within two or three generations: it was no less than a revolution and a crisis.[71] The increasing population growth was experienced amid several other fundamental commotions – of war, famine and clearance. Population was growing faster than at any time before or since. It was creating an impossible burden on the old system. As Donald Winch remarks, 'One way of bringing this home to present-day

material becomes fuller after 1650, it depicts a society sinking more and more into a condition of overpopulation, manifesting all the dysfunctions one expect under the circumstances.' Problems were compounded after 1650 and the tacksmen were regarded as particularly oppressive. R.A. Dodgshon, *Land and Society in Early Scotland* (Oxford: Clarendon Press, 1981), pp. 277, 285.

71   The population increases were visited on a relatively poor society which was already vulnerable to short-term mortality crises. Eric Cregeen made no bones about the levels of poverty in the old Highlands: the commoners' diet was based on oats and barley, and fish and dairy produce, with rarely any meat. A recourse to shellfish was common in the late seventeenth century. He cites the effects of the incursions of sand from strong winds: 'Traditions existed in the late eighteenth century that all the population of the extensive district of Brolas in Mull perished except a few families'. Eric Cregeen, 'Tradition and Change', in *Recollections of an Argyllshire Drover and Other West Highland Chronicles* (Edinburgh: John Donald, 2004), p. 254. Visitors were commonly shocked at conditions: thus in 1784 J. A. Knox remarked that Highland estates were 'seats of oppression, famine, anguish and despair.' Quoted in Dodgshon, *Land and Society*, p.319. Dr Johnson was, famously, a less appalled and also a more credible witness.

readers is to ask them to consider the likely effect on the current political agenda if the British population had doubled during the period between 1950 and 2000'.[72]

Coping with population increase was an overwhelming problem, with numbers growing at an astonishing rate, often pushing towards more intensive settlements along the coasts, smaller lots, individualised and congested crofts, sometimes associated with new model villages developed to create income, accommodation and employment.[73] The incursion of large-scale pastoralism was built on top of this – expanding income horizons for the region. The factor's job became much more complicated.

It is clear that, across the Highlands, the population growth took place with little restraint, growing spectacularly even when thousands of men were away in the regiments during the French Wars. The landlords in general seem to have actively encouraged population growth until about 1810. The people themselves did not take control over their own reproduction – which is scarcely surprising since no European country had grasped this problem.[74] These changes

72   See D. Winch, 'Introduction', in D. Winch and P.K. O'Brien, *The Political Economy of British Historical Experience 1688-1914* (Oxford: Oxford University Press for the British Academy, 2002), p.7, fn. 8.

73   Dodgshon chronicles the elimination of touns across Scotland, and the general re-organisation of tenancies which often entailed the widespread shedding of cottar populations and subtenants across Scotland. The reclamation of mosses was a means often devised to absorb displaced people on the muirs. Robert Dodgshon, 'The Clearances and the transformation of the Scottish countryside,' in *The Oxford Handbook of Modern Scottish History*, edited by T.M. Devine and Jenny Wormald (Oxford: Oxford University Press, 2012).

74   There is a parallel debate concerning the demographic factor regarding the transformation of the English peasantry in the sixteenth and seventeenth centuries, made famous in the work of R.H. Tawney. One side of the argument entailed the idealisation of the virtues of the sturdy independent yeomanry who were 'murdered by greed, folly, and cowardice of landlords, lawyers and government'. The outcome was that it 'left the rural poor exposed to the full pressures of ruthless capitalist agriculture.' It was ultimately a

amounted to a structural transformation, a massive redeployment of the much larger population and a revolution in land use for sheep – which was ultimately expressed in the Clearances.

During these tumultuous times the factor was, of course, also responsible for the financial viability of the estates, that is, their survival in the hands of the current proprietor. Over and over again the factors were required to press for, and extract, higher rents in order to balance the conspicuous consumption behaviour of their employers – exacerbated by absenteeism, massive capital expenditure on houses, external travel and living arrangements.[75] The factors were constantly battling against the hazard of bankruptcy. And many of them failed – hence the extraordinary turnover in Highland estate ownership throughout this crisis.[76] The factors were usually in the invidious position of counterbalancing the extravagance of their proprietors. This conflict particularly related to the estates which lacked sources of external cross-subsidies. Estate management was practised in a highly unstable context, especially at the end of the

moral judgement. An alternative view stresses the 'critical importance of demographic growth as a destabilising factor' which entailed 'the relentless demographic growth which multiplied the number of villages until the pressure on the land became acute.' According to Lawrence Stone, 'Population pressure has replaced the wicked enclosing and rack renting landlords as the *diabolus ex machina*.' Lawrence Stone, introduction to *The Agrarian Problem in the Sixteenth Century*, by R.H. Tawney (New York: Harper Torchbooks, 1967), pp. vii-xi.

75 See for instance Ian H. Adams (ed.), *Papers on Peter May, Land Surveyor, 1749-1793* (Edinburgh: Scottish History Society, 1979), Introduction, pp.-xvii. It is perhaps significant that there seems to have been little criticism of chieftainly extravagance in earlier times – see Cregeen, *Recollections*, p. 254.

76 Absenteeism, of course, enhanced the role and responsibilities of the factors – men, according to Hunter, who 'had all the power in their own hands'. They were thereby exposed to the greatest temptations. He quotes an observation in 1813 that their situation was 'greater than a man of ordinary virtue and fortitude can resist.' James Hunter, *The Making of a Crofting Community*, New edn. (Edinburgh: Birlinn, 2010), p.174.

Napoleonic Wars when prices of many Highland commodities collapsed. It became a switchback of economic conditions, great lurches in the fortunes of the component parts of the new economy, in all the sectors – fishing, textiles, slate, coal, kelp, wool, cotton and flax. None of this was exclusive to the Highlands, but the concentrated combination of adversities was chronic.

Factors were therefore most often saddled with the task of rescuing or repairing the estate finances in conditions of landlord extravagance and over-commitment and/or of falling rental income. Usually this required the use of managerial scissors – that is, reducing expenditure with one blade, extracting more income with the other. Neither made for popularity with either the tenantry or the employer. At the other extreme of Highland estate management, factors were sometimes required to supervise immense expenditures on new infrastructure and estate improvements, for instance, new building programmes, new enterprises, new villages, new roads, resettlement sites, and, of course, the relocation or dispersal of the small tenantry. In some cases these expenditures were extremely large and onerous. The Sutherland estate was exceptional: here there was an expenditure of more than £1 million over a period of twenty-two years (1811-33) – equivalent in the 2015 terms of more than £55 million[77] – and much more in later decades. But there were other estates, famously under Matheson and later Leverhulme in Lewis, which also pursued extraordinarily expensive investment/improvement policies which, by their sheer scale, strained the capacity of their factors/managers.

The factor therefore became the channel, the conduit, which transmitted the strain from the top to the bottom of the system which, in the last resort, ended with the eviction

77   These were figures claimed by James Loch in 1833: see Eric Richards, *Leviathan of Wealth* (London: Routledge, 1973), p.259.

of small tenants in order to accommodate the introduction of higher paying sheep farmers and, later, sporting tenants. Meanwhile the owners would blame the factors for unpopularity and mismanagement, rarely relating it to their own demands. Part of the trouble was that the factor had also to cover old duties left over from previous times. This included recruiting for regiments, maintaining political influence and preserving religious conformity.[78]

Across these decades there were many symptoms of stress and strain among the managerial *corps* as they faced the scale and the enormity of the changes they were required to impose upon the region. Some of the factors showed signs of great hesitation and personal distress at the prospect and the actuality of the changes. Often they confronted contradictory commands in circumstances which offered few solutions.

---

78   In 1841 three-quarters of all Highland proprietors were non-resident. See *First Report from the Select Committee on Emigration, Scotland, 1841*, evidence of Dr Norman Macleod, pp. 867-71, and 808, in *British Parliamentary Papers* (Shannon: Irish University Press, 1968). The size of estates increased and so did the pace of turnover. The factors became the main agents of change – they had to manage the restructuring of the region, often in the face of vociferous opposition and ambivalent or pusillanimous owners who wanted the changes without the opprobrium. This was their burden and they received little credit.

VIII

The Argyll Estates

The individual behaviour of particular factors inevitably focuses on personal characteristics, and this might easily become a recital of the personal foibles and behaviour of certain individuals, some with a grim record of oppression. Accounting for the general reputation of the entire class of Highland factors requires a broader view of the conditions under which they worked and the circumstances and temptations that set a framework on their role in Highland society.[79] Nevertheless some concrete cases help to define the circumstances and responses of these men who effectively were responsible for so much of the actual transformation of the Highlands in the late eighteenth and the early nineteenth centuries. This was the work of the Highland estate factor during the long crisis as defined above. Moreover the factor's life and thinking was often self-recorded in the well-organised estate papers, especially in the larger aristocratic estates, of which a handful of examples

---

79   On the role of individual responsibility and the broader determinants in historical explanations see for instance, the remarks of E.H. Carr, quoted in Jonathan Haslam, *The Vices of Integrity: E.H. Carr, 1892-1982* (London: Verso, 1999), p. 198.

can be cited here. Some of these examples bring to light the frequently invidious and conflicted position of the estate administrators in times of radical change as determined by the old and the new owners of the great estates.

The turmoil on the island of Tiree, on the great Argyll estates, has been splendidly documented by the late Eric Cregeen. Here the pace and direction of 'Improvement' was determined by the dukes – thus the second Duke of Argyll had already abolished clan tenures in Mull in 1737 and introduced modern leases – leading towards rack-renting.[80] His successors after 1743 attempted to introduce modernisation across the estates: this commonly entailed the abolition of the semi-communal system of runrig, the institution of enclosures, new crops, tree planting, new drainage methods, larger consolidated farms, and investment on new roads. There were also ambitious plans for new villages to accommodate the landless population to be displaced by the abolition of runrig, and often associated with the sudden expansion of kelp manufacture from the 1780s. The long-term ducal intention was to concentrate the population in villages and to employ the land in larger farms.[81] It was a programme of Improvement, and it required robust removal and relocation policies.[82]

The central fact of the Argyll context was the immense growth of population: the number of people living on Tiree increased from 1,500 in 1747 to 2,770 in 1802, and then

---

80 Leases gave much better control over the land and this was widely recognised as a controlling device across the world of improvement agriculture. Robert Young, a Morayshire land steward, made this point explicitly in 1811: 'Farming and improvement cannot be carried on without the command of lands', by which he meant leases. Quoted in Douglas G. Lockhart (ed.), *Scottish Planned Villages* (Edinburgh: Scottish History Society, 2012), p. 3.

81 There were also financial considerations which required sales in 1776 of Ulva and Morven, sales which were followed by Clearances.

82 See Cregeen, *Recollections*, p. 259.

to 4,453 by 1831. Astonishingly the population continued to rise to 5,000 by 1861. The managers of Argyll were faced with a community which was expanding rapidly, but was still glued to the old runrig system and the old methods of cultivation.

The Duke determined to relocate and to re-fix the people: that is, shifting most of them out to villages on the coast while the old interior land would be re-set to more substantial individual farms. The outcome for the landlord would be greatly enhanced rental income from all parts of the tenantry. The sheer scale and optimism of these plans is impressive but it was also a recipe for turmoil, conflict and various sorts of resistance – all of which had to be shouldered and orchestrated by the factors. Meantime the position of the factor himself had been redefined. The Argyll estates over the years from 1770 to 1806 were operated through an agent in Edinburgh who issued instructions from the Duke to the chamberlains on the estates, increasingly known as 'factors'. The hereditary chamberlains had been displaced and the new men possessed less status but higher salaries, reduced privileges, less power, less independence and were subject to better auditors. They were part of the development of 'a salaried bureaucracy'. And with the abolition of the tacksmen their duties were greater. Cregeen draws a comparison with Russia in 1791, where the old aristocratic bailiffs were replaced by humbler men. The new factors had to cope with the changing orders of the Duke, directives from above. The factors had minimal influence except to suggest problems. It was neither an attractive nor a popular role.

The assault on the tacksmen came early in the eighteenth century – cutting out the middlemen, itself a source of continuing resentment in the community. This change was associated with the institution of competitive bidding for leases, which became the norm. The 'Ducal improvements went forward … amidst a population largely hostile to the changes'. There was a diametrical opposition of old and new, of tradition and modernity, of change and resistance. The Duke was forcing through his plans which soon aroused opposition in many forms. Already in the 1750s there was strong resentment brewing. In 1756 the Duke declared: 'I am resolved to keep no tenants but such as will be peaceable and supply industry.' He required the kirk ministers to announce this after their Sunday sermons. In 1771 the Chamberlain of the Argyll estate spoke of the 'the insolence and outrage to which they [the tenants] are naturally prone' – and identified a degree of incitement by 'the lesser gentry', almost certainly meaning the displaced tacksmen of the old system.[83]

The pressure was clearly transmitted from above and channelled through the factors/chamberlains. But part of their responsibility was to ensure continuing loyalty amongst the subtenants and the various family connections. Cregeen was emphatic that the factors were placed in an invidious position – mediating between the zeal and sophisticated tastes of the Duke and the gentlemen farmers on the one side, and the traditional values of the population at large on the other. This tension bred passive resistance and the withholding of co-operation at all levels.

The Duke's determination was redoubled in the 1780s and 90s when a further major restructuring of the old society was being pressed upon the islanders. This was powerfully generated by the great boom in kelp production which provided astonishing new employment opportunities for the

---

83   Quoted by E. Cregeen, 'The Changing Role of the House of Argyll in the Scottish Highlands', in N.T. Phillipson, and Rosalind Mitchison (eds), *Scotland in the Age of the Improvement* (Edinburgh: Edinburgh University Press, 1970), p. 10

North Uist eviction, 1895. (Reproduced by permission of Comann Eachdraidh Uibhist a Tuath)

Evander MacIver,
Scourie Factor.

John Mackenzie, Doctor,
Factor and Farmer in Gairloch
and Easter Ross, 1803-1886.

John Munro Mackenzie, the diarist and Chamberlain of the Lews.
(Reproduced by permission of the Mackenzie family)

Donald Munro, Chamberlain of the Lews
(Reproduced by permission of
Colin Scott Mackenzie)

Robert Charles
Carrington, Factor at
Dunkeld, 1837-58.
(Courtesy of Atholl
Estates)

John Robertson, Factor at Blair, 1863-1902.
(Courtesy of Atholl Estates)

'The Factor's Reckoning', North Uist, 1891. (Reproduced by permission of Comann Eachdraidh Uibhist a Tuath)

Patrick Sellar. (Reproduced by permission of the National Library of Scotland)

James Loch, 1780-1855. Commissioner of the Sutherland Estates, 1812 to 1855. (© National Portrait Gallery, London)

The 'careworn' Captain Boycott. (© The British Library Board. NEWS12005)

Captain Boycott and his escort. (© The British Library Board. 4211.220000)

coastal communities. The Duke of Argyll made great efforts to staunch emigration, instituting plans of improvement to retain the people not only in kelp production but also in the expansion of the villages, in fishing, and the development of industrial initiatives. He now exuded an unquenchable optimism. It was a time 'when it seemed still possible to divert the best of industry from the lowland concentrations, to irrigate the highland with channels of new wealth to keep the Highlanders at home.'[84] According to Cregeen this was 'the best conceived attempt before the deluge of the nineteenth century … to preserve the Scottish Highlands from depopulation and decay.' It was pursued in tandem with the ongoing effort to convert the estates from runrig into large consolidated farms. This was also the root of great opposition in the Tiree community, which eventually overturned the policy. The context therefore was one of structural transformation pressed upon the unwilling community from above. The place of the factors in this turmoil was symptomatic of the intrinsic conflict.

From 1770 to 1799 the factors or chamberlains were all Campbells. Donald Campbell, son of a tacksman of Mull, was a substantial figure who 'presided over the destinies of the Tiree people.' He was heir to the 'old time chamberlains'. The factors indeed were conspicuously conservative figures: Campbell was essentially 'out of sympathy with improvement

---

84   Eric Cregeen (ed.), *Argyll Estate Instructions*, p. xxxxviii. On Skye in the late 1790s, Lord Macdonald employed a new factor, John Blackadder, a Berwickshire land surveyor and a carrier of new methods. On the Urquhart estate in the 1790-1810 period, he experienced managerial quandaries when emigration seemed to threaten the advance of kelp production. Blackadder wanted to introduce new methods and to increase rents but was aware of the conservatism of the population, remarking that 'no man gives up readily what he has without a substitute equal or better.' He was also anxious not to precipitate emigration and he advocated subdivision of lots as essential to keep the population to levels necessary for kelp production. See J.M. Bumsted, *The People's Clearance: Highland Emigration to British North America, 1770-1815* (Edinburgh: Edinburgh University Press, 1982), p. 85.

and the development of the estate on modern lines.' He was regarded by the Duke as obstructive, as an agent of restraint, wanting to retain the status quo.'[85]

It is abundantly clear that the Duke wanted to act as the benign proprietor but also sought to increase his rents in line with general trends (in part to deal with his own financial confusion and the danger of bankruptcy). His Edinburgh Improvement advisors, the experts who deplored the old system and offered a new model, had captured the attention of the Duke.

The people of Tiree set themselves against all change. This was 'the peasant mentality,' according to Cregeen: 'The tenants were strongly against giving up their traditional methods, notably runrig.' In between was the chamberlain, the factor, who though possessing local knowledge, was expected to follow the plan instituted by the Duke and his Edinburgh mentors. The Tiree story twisted and turned, but it is clear that the factors themselves were in a cleft stick; they were professionally beholden to the proprietor to make the system work (even under radical change imposed from above), and yet felt responsible for the welfare of the people. Often the two obligations were diametrically opposed.

The rising tension of the community was thus mediated through the conflicted figure of the factor: in Tiree the Duke and the factor were at odds; the Duke wanted more of the profits derived from kelp and the improvement of yields. He blamed his factor for his inability to extract better rents:[86] the factor was chastised for allowing the tenants to squander their profits from kelp on drink and inefficiency.[87] In effect

---

85 E.A. Cregeen, *Recollections*, p. 23. James Boswell met the Duke of Argyll's factor on Tiree in 1773 and described him as 'a genteel, agreeable man.' *Journal of a Tour to the Hebrides* (2000 edition), p.301.

86 Ibid, p. 29.

87 Ibid, p. 38.

the 'old time chamberlains' were tied to the old system.[88] They were operating as a brake on the Duke's own rationalising plans and in 1794 he was told that the tenants simply could not pay the rent increases that he demanded; in response the Duke blamed the factor for neglecting improvement. Indeed the factors strongly opposed the Duke's plans for small consolidated farms and the abolition of runrig as totally impractical. The factors were advocating the opposite policy – that is, the redistribution of land to fit the people's needs, taking into account the swollen population and the great number of the supernumeraries in the communities of cottars. The Duke was angrily critical of the agent for allowing 'the tenants to drink their barley and squander the other productions of the land', and their dependence exclusively on kelp to pay their rents.

Consequently there was great conflict between the Duke and his managers though the latter were required to execute the Duke's plans.[89] As time passed the problems of implementing the plan of reorganisation mounted. The island was reported to be 'on the verge of revolt'.[90] The tenants were strongly against giving up their traditional methods. There was uproar and the threat of widespread emigration. At the start of 1803 the plans were in limbo, the factors blamed on both sides for the tumult on the island.

Suddenly, in October 1803, the Duke changed his mind, apparently induced to do so by the threat of emigration – and the thirty-year-old plan was reversed. The Duke had performed a *volte face*, the perfect somersault – and eventually he ordered a large-scale subdivision of the lands to make crofts. This inevitably caused further aggravation among the local tacksmen who were the losers by the

---

88 Ibid p. 23.

89 Ibid p. 28.

90 Ibid p. 34.

reversal. The factors were given no credit in these gyrations, though their role had been entirely conservative throughout.[91]

The outcome on Tiree was a triumph of the people and the defeat of the plans for Improvement. The resort to subdivision to accommodate the people was made possible by the profits of kelp which persisted until 1815. In the long run however the denser island population had been encouraged and here, as elsewhere on the Argyll estates, subdivision and crofting were instituted. Ultimately the result was chronic congestion.

The next generation of factors had to deal with the collapse of kelp production and the immense tide of emigration and the end of optimism. Eventually many of the Argyll estate lands were sold off and clearances followed. When the problems of congestion and poverty mounted the factor declared that the Duke had favoured the growth of population and the subdivision of the farms. By then 'conflict was the normal condition of his [the Duke's] relations with the chamberlain.' According to Cregeen, 'The chamberlain was always on the side of the tenants, striving to protect them from what appeared to him to be wrong'.

The factor's role in these transitions was painfully discordant: that is, they had to implement deeply unpopular policies on a resistant population, while unconvinced of the changes, and were then required to administer the consequences of the Duke's *volte face*.[92]

---

91   Ibid p. 35.

92   E.A. Cregeen, 'The Changing Role of the House of Argyll', p. 22 fn 8.

IX

Assynt

The displacement of the tacksmen in estate affairs and their role in encouraging emigration were deeply contentious elements in estate administration and their consequences reverberated over many decades. The Assynt estate in Sutherland in the 1770s is well documented and here the role of the factor became central in the impending changes. There was nothing new about the factor's unpopularity: it was a dangerous occupation. In 1737, for instance, there had been violence against estate officials at a rent collection and Calder House was fired.[93]

At this stage the new estate factors were explicitly trying to counter the influence of the tacksmen and their much-reported oppressions. The latter had been abusing their tacks and rack renting, and this was given as the reason for their replacement and the institution of direct renting by the landlord. The middlemen were thus ousted and were later accused, notably in 1772, of inciting the small tenantry to emigrate.[94] The factors deplored emigration and blamed the

---

93   R.J. Adam (ed.), *Home's Survey of Assynt*, p. xii.

94   Ibid, p. xxiv. Ian Grimble, in *The World of Rob Donn*, revised edn

tacksmen. From this time forward there was severe tension between the factors and the tacksmen and their descendants. It was a continuing animosity which eventually poisoned social relations, and created a mutinous layer of antagonists who fomented trouble on the estate for decades to come. There was a notable eruption against Patrick Sellar when he attempted to execute removals from his new sheep farms in 1813/14.

Assynt factors were aware of the prospects for sheep farming as early as 1775 and were interested in making a trial: but they were conservative in attitude and nothing was set going for another twenty-five years. Their tasks included dealing with famine in 1772 and the fear of starvation. Factors made desperate efforts to bring relief supplies to the people: they created work for relief and shipped in grain from Caithness and Ross. Meanwhile, however, the threat of emigration had become a bargaining chip to reduce rents.[95] Relief expenditure in 1772 amounted to £2,200 out of a rental of £3,000; the financial mess caused one factor to emigrate himself.

Another experiment in estate management was performed in the east of Sutherland when George Dempster, the

---

(Edinburgh: Saltire Society, 1999) used emigrant testimonies of 1773-75 to demonstrate that factors and tacksmen were lining their own pockets at the expense of the people; and meanwhile opulent graziers were ingrossing farms and causing turmoil among the old tenants who became increasingly suggestible to the idea of emigration.

95   Adam, *Home's Survey*, p. xxvii. Tacksmen oppressing the sub-tenantry in the 1770s and the 1780s is also documented by Andrew Mackillop who points out that this was the standard reason given by the middle tenantry for their decisions to emigrate at that time. It was also the common reason given by landlords for obliterating the tacksmen class from their estate systems. This was a policy widely followed across the Highlands in the late eighteenth century, but it was not uniform. On some estates there was a clear recognition that the tacksmen were the most effective deliverers of rental income and management and some estates saw them as indispensable. See Andrew Mackillop, *'More Fruitful than the Soil': Army, Empire and the Scottish Highlands, 1715-1815* (East Linton: Tuckwell, 2000), pp. 171-73.

arch-improver from the south, bought the Skibo estate in 1786, a century before Andrew Carnegie. He introduced entirely new schemes for working the land and rearranged the land and its tenantry. Dempster appointed as factor, John Fraser, the son of an Inverness vintner with much local knowledge. He was expected to transpose Dempster's success at Dunnichen in Angus into the north eastern lands of Sutherland. Fraser was given great authority but became very critical of the conditions he faced at Skibo. He eventually found himself overstretched and was succeeded as factor by Mackay of Torboll who seemed to achieve better results. Dempster himself was a passionate improver and notably detested the traditional use of labour services and wanted their abolition. He was indeed critical of his larger neighbours, the Gowers of the great Sutherland estate. Dempster was a friend of the family but he did not want them to return 'to those disgraceful days when the factor called 50 men from their own work in Kildonan to work in the gardens at Dunrobin [and] sent them home again, unfed and unpaid.'[96]

Managerial changes were occurring across the entire region but especially in the south east of the Highlands. In the more favoured low lying lands of the Black Isle, improvements were being been forced onwards by local proprietors with the aid of factors, mainly Lowlanders. Several owners, early in the eighteenth century, were already creating single farms out of runrigs, converting services and produce rents into formal cash rents. This process required enclosures and the displacement of the people. Here there was serious resistance: in 1727 more than 500 people rioted against the changes. The tenants of Sir Thomas Urquhart – 'the ancient tenantrie' – considered any move from their native farmtoun

96   John Evans, *Gentleman Usher* (Barnsley: Pen and Sword Military, 2004), pp. 186, 309.

as equal to exile in Barbados or Madagascar. The local estate factors regarded their dealings with small tenants as a penance and a severe burden – it was 'near slavery,' said Sir John Sinclair. Their work was much more difficult than that of their counterparts in the south of Scotland where factoring was a 'sinecure'. Consequently the profession tended to attract strong personalities. The dynamic factor of Strachan in 1849 was known for his 'tyrannical oppression': he was described as 'full of vainglory and void of all principle,' evicting and refusing all compensation. He brought in new farmers from outside: there was 'the new class of factors and commercial farmers' and the social fabric was being rent.[97]

By the 1820s and 30s the great Sutherland estate sprawled across the northern Highlands but was also connected to large and complex family estates in England: it required an elaborate hierarchy of managers, from its 'Commissioner' down to its local ground officers. There was a recurring circulation of factors/agents between the English and Scottish estates belonging to the Sutherland empire. Francis Suther had begun on the Trentham estate in Staffordshire in 1813/14 after serving Sir John Henderson: he was described as 'mild and gentlemanlike', and a good penman and was employed on a salary of £200 pa with a horse and house provided. In September 1816 he was sent north to Sutherland to take over from the increasingly rancorous and dysfunctional management of William Young and Patrick Sellar. Suther presided over massive clearances in 1819-21 and was under great strain. He died in in October 1824, succeeded by George Gunn. There was in reality a two-way flow of managerial expertise, with a substantial net movement

---

97 David Alston, *My Little Town of Cromarty* (Edinburgh: Birlinn, 2006), pp. 252, 199.

southwards.[98] For instance, William Lewis from Fife had been trained in the south of Scotland and then succeeded Suther on the English estates of the Sutherland family; after two decades of service his health broke down and he died from overwork.[99] The central administration of the Sutherland estates had keen qualms about the involvement of so many Scots in the management of the English estates – there was a concern that they might be regarded as foreigners.[100] They were on big salaries, and top estate agents were poached by rival estates, and often sought increased salaries and extra perquisites.

98   On the preference for non-locals and questions of training and salaries see Tindley, 'They sow...', pp. 68-77.

99   See Wordie, *Town and Countryside*, p. 73.

100 Ibid., p. 65.

X

The Seaforth Case[101]

The situation of the Seaforth Estate in the 1790s was decidedly complicated and the factorship was mesmerised by the behaviour of the owner. The new laird of the Seaforth Estate, the fifth earl, displayed a profoundly divided personality and philosophy: he had lived most of his life in England but was passionately committed to acting the part of the traditional clan chief. He was an oddly constructed Highlander – in effect, an Englishman who had adopted all the trappings and notions of the old clan chieftainship. He regarded his mission as that of retaining his hereditary clan lands while also sustaining the swelling estate population. None of this was consistent with his grandiose ideas of social status and personal expenditure, and this contradiction caused his managers severe problems over several decades.

The trouble was that Seaforth's income was much less than his living expenses: he insisted on displaying his elevated

---

101 This section is heavily indebted to the work of Finlay McKichan, 'Lord Seaforth and Highland Estate Management in the first phase of clearance (1783-1815),' *Scottish Historical Review*, v.86, 2007; Finlay McKichan 'Lord Seaforth: Highland proprietor, Caribbean governor and slave owner,' *idem*, v. 90: 2 (Oct. 2011).

status as a great political and society figure in the north and in the south. He desperately wanted to maintain his customary role, his traditional clan relations and his political influence. He made the greatest play of his patriarchal pride and his commitment to raising regiments.

Seaforth owned estates on mainland Ross and on Lewis and when his finances deteriorated, he was advised to sell off Lochalsh and Kintail and invest more fully in the Lewis properties. But Seaforth was confused and inconsistent and his factors were repeatedly hamstrung, while the finances of the estate continued to deteriorate.[102]

At all points Seaforth invoked his clan responsibilities over economic rationality. As he said in 1788, 'as common business I would sell these estates, but as a head of Family and of a Clan, I would not'. A few years later he spoke warmly of 'proprietors who are often under the necessity of sacrificing their own interest' in order to provide for their population: such lairds had resisted the temptations of sheep farming (and evictions). Yet Seaforth recognised the contradictions of his position, observing that the old runrig system of occupying the lands made little sense and that 'a conjunct farm is a cantonment of wretches who quarrel together', yet 'to dismiss all supernumeraries is a harsh remedy.'[103]

Seaforth always proclaimed what he called 'the incomprehensible feeling by which we are led to value antiquity of family and permanence of property.' His entire strategy was to avoid the sale of his estates and to retain the population on his estates at least in part because regimental recruitment ultimately depended on the estate population.[104]

---

102 See also John Macdonald, *A History of Lewis* (1978), pp. 34, 88, 95, 118, 133.

103 Finlay McKichan 'Lord Seaforth: Highland proprietor, Caribbean governor and slave owner,' *idem*, v. 90: 2 (Oct. 2011), p. 53.

104 The idea that the factor had to guard the dignity of the laird was captured by Lord MacDonald's factor in 1803, opposing emigration, on

Thus Seaforth was endlessly equivocating over the issue of modernising his estates. He wanted to avoid the common response of proprietors like the Macleods of Glengarry who had doubled and trebled their rents by introducing sheep farmers, which then precipitated widespread emigration. Seaforth's factors were in a quandary and at least as conflicted as Seaforth. One of them (from a succession of factors from the family of Gillanders), in the 1790s opposed the sale of some of the mainland estates to pay off debts on the grounds that they were part of the family's ancient patrimony:

> they having been in the family's property for centuries
> … they are the flower of
>
> Highlanders, and what our ancestors would have
> purchased with blood and treasure.

In this case the factor reasserted romance and sentiment over economic efficiency. Of several possible strategies the same factor recommended a renewed recruitment of his tenants for the regiment. The factor in Lewis urged Seaforth onward: 'your military successes will dissolve all necessity of parting with the Lewis'.[105] Recruiting promised to bolster estate revenues by expanding external income flowing into the estate, simultaneously of course encouraging a larger population. The trouble was that much of this feeling was not reciprocated – the actual recruitment for the regiments was poor and Seaforth lamented that 'all feudal ideas in short are quite vanished and gone.'

Another solution was a compromise advocated by his factors. They suggested that Seaforth undertake a partial sale of some of his lands: thus he could sell off Glensheil

---

the grounds that it was 'beneath the dignity' of his lordship 'to yield to a few restless, infatuated people'. Quoted by James Hunter in *Making of the Crofting Community*, p. 56.

105 McKichan, op. cit. p.60.

and introduce a few sheep farmers; this would secure a handsome augmentation of rents and enable Seaforth to retain most of his small tenants. The factors advised that sheep farming could be consistent with 'continuing your tenants'. The plan entailed a combination of increased subdivision (made feasible by the expansion of kelp making on the shores, contingent on continuing kelp revenues), increased rents and limited clearances – all in the name of compromise. Seaforth's reluctance was derived from his traditionalist philosophy, clan sentiment acting as a brake. But the factors also argued that the threat to introduce outsiders as sheep farmers might induce existing tenants to pay greatly increased rents. Seaforth continued to resist, correctly predicting that the introduction of sheep farming would precipitate emigration from his estates.

Another strategy of survival was that of seeking a colonial appointment and/or slave estates in the West Indies. Seaforth expected to restore his fortunes by buying a slave plantation in Berbice to raise cotton and, in 1801, taking on a colonial governorship. His plan was to avoid selling off his lands in Wester Ross – partly out of fear that any new owner would convert to sheep and 'dispeople' the same estates. The plan was to raise enough income from the West Indies to cross-subsidise the hereditary estates in the West Highlands and Islands.[106] It was a common enough strategy among Highland proprietors in the late eighteenth century and some were phenomenally successful. But for Seaforth the plan turned into miserable failure.

Ultimately all these strategies failed and the problems of the estate finances moved towards total disarray. The factors were fed contradictory or compromising instructions,

---

106 Here he was following a substantial example of the Malcolms of Poltalloch, the Frasers of Belladrum (near Beauly), and the Bailies of Dochfour.

frequently impossible to implement, but they were liable for all responsibility on all sides. In the event Seaforth's own extravagance and poor management of the estate led inevitably to impossible debts followed by land sales. His factors looked on askance; at his extravagance, his contradictions and his deteriorating finances. His expenditures rose madly as he played out his assumed chieftainly roles while the finances of the estates failed to meet his needs. The estate finances fell into a mess, uncontrollable by the factors.[107] The end result was final failure – overpopulation, bankruptcy and ultimately land sales. Moreover when the land was sold the final result was that which Seaforth had sought so passionately to avoid – namely clearances and evictions.[108]

Atavistic notions pervaded the mentality of estate owners at large in the late eighteenth century. Moreover Highland estates, when the heir was under age or away in the war or on colonial service, often employed trustees and commissioners. They were required to increase income: thus, for instance, John Blackadder on Lord MacDonald's estates in Skye recommended 'new and better customs and methods of management' to increase rents. But he also recommended the conservation of the population and advised that the

---

107 Of the factors the Gillanders were the most significant in the late eighteenth century and the family became something of a dynasty of factors. Despite the extreme difficulties of managing the Seaforth estates, George Gillanders eventually retired in 1796, having been successful enough to buy his own estate at Highfield. Peter Fairbairn, who first succeeded the Gillanders, was less influential – and was sent to Berbice to manage the plantations. He was succeeded by his own son Alexander. Later James Gillanders of Highfield was responsible for infamous Clearances in Glencalvie and Strathconon. Much of the executive business of the estate was placed in the hands of an Edinburgh lawyer whose critical task was to negotiate Seaforth's debts.

108 See Finlay McKichan, op. cit., passim. The distinction between clearances and eviction is often slippery. People 'cleared' were sometimes peacefully resettled on an estate; forcible eviction was the fate of uncooperative tenants who were ejected without alternative provision. 'Removal' was a variant, usually in the context of relocation.

estate should move slowly since 'no man gives up readily what he has without a substitute equal or better.' He feared generating emigration, in a kelping context, and advocated subdivision as a means of maintaining the population. Similarly, Sir James Grant, factor at Urquhart in 1801, was very fearful of emigration, yet did not know how to stop it. He offered longer leases but found that the threat of emigration was being used as a lever by the crofters to resist rent increases.[109]

---

109 Bumsted, *People's Clearance*, pp. 85-88.

XI

Atholl's Factors

The factors on the Atholl estates also faced managerial problems precipitated by the extravagance of the owner. The Atholl finances were undermined by temptations encountered by the Duke in Perth and, more likely, in London. Such was 'not at all unusual for the nobility of the period.'

On the Atholl estate the tacksman/agency system was traditionally based on kinship, which was gradually eroded by the introduction of single-tenancy arrangements and short leases, and the conversion of labour services and produce rents into money rents. After 1741 there was much more professionalism – and the factors were able to exercise clear powers to evict tenants in arrears. By then the factor system had been introduced, supported by a class of sub-factors, a new regime which was associated with sustained rent increases through the period from 1732 to 1788, all of which long predated sheep clearances.

The Duke of Atholl was evidently ambivalent about the modernising changes he was imposing. In 1772 he wrote to the Duke of Gordon pointing out that their wealth and rank 'has been purchased by the blood of the ancestors of our present dependants and tenants. We ought to live and let live.' Yet Atholl was already in the middle of squeezing rents upwards in a radical fashion. In Highland estate management in the second half of the eighteenth century there was a widespread and recurring tension between commercial aspirations and traditions of paternalism, and the strains were commonly mediated by the factors with mixed success.[110]

On the Atholl estates the modernising tendencies strengthened as the decades passed. Increasingly any factor found to be less than stringent was under critical scrutiny by the Duke. Lesser landowners acted as factors – thus in the Dunkeld district during the 1790s the fourth Duke of Atholl was served by Robert Stewart of Garth. He was ill-tempered and arbitrary though full of hospitality. In 1795 he was sacked: he had been incompetent in rearranging the estate. The Duke told him, 'you have not got the capacity for energy and exertion which is requisite in a person who has the charge of an estate such as mine.'[111] Any factor found ineffective or insufficiently zealous in performing the landlord's wishes faced the obvious hazard of dismissal. Again, in 1817, the Duke replaced one factor with another who was more likely to clear old tenants: factors were simply sacked if they failed to toe the line. Of one such factor it was remarked that he was 'a most judicious honourable country gentleman who declared that he could not in good conscience follow up the measures proscribed.' He was then dismissed, and replaced by 'a man totally ignorant of the people, their language, their character, their habits ... totally ignorant of the history of the country, its produce and its

110 Leneman, *Living in Atholl*, pp. 11, 15, 17, 20, 25, 19.

111 Quoted in James Irvine Robertson, *The First Highlander: Major-General David Stewart of Garth* (East Linton: Tuckwell, 1998), p. 12.

soil.' In this case the new man was substituted for 'an honourable ... country gentleman whose object was to do justice to landlord and tenant.'[112]

It is likely that, as the demands for structural change in the worsening Highland crisis increased, the less forceful and the weak-willed among the factors were cumulatively weeded out in favour of rigorous men who could force through change with greater efficacy and stringency. Thus the relatively benign proprietor and improver, Dr John Mackenzie, dismissed his own manager because he 'was unfit for it from want of firmness of character and [of] over good nature.' He was replaced by a man from Skye – employed on account of 'his firmness of disposition', and capacity to put a stop to certain 'socialistic rights of tenantry superseding those of a landlord, which evil disposed persons had been sowing among minds of the discontented,' and 'those who would no doubt have preferred being entirely idle.'[113]

Dr John Mackenzie commonly referred to the crofters and cottars as 'the small people'. He was however highly critical of non-Gaelic-speaking factors who despised the crofter: 'No wonder ... that with that common breed of factors, crofters don't move ahead – and are eagerly exchanged, by evictions by the score, for one English speaking, rich absentee sheep farmer'. He was referring specifically to his 'old friend' Peter Brown, factor of the estate of Munro of Novar. Mackenzie himself was fluent in Gaelic.[114]

Most factors were generally assumed to be 'hostile to the small tenants'. Thus Donald Robertson, factor on the

---

112 Ibid. p.89.

113 J. Mackenzie, *Letter to Lord John Russell on Sir John McNeill's Report on the State of the West Highlands and Islands of Scotland* (Edinburgh: W. Blackwood, 1851), p. 27.

114 Christina Byam Shaw, *Pigeon Holes of Memory*, p. 253.

Chisholm Estates, in 1825 identified smuggling and subletting as the main problems in his management: he remarked that 'while these two evils are allowed to be practised, the people will continue to be poor and miserable and of course uncontrollable, and will not think of turning their attention to any other employment for their own support.'[115]

The Clearances were the most obvious test of the mettle of a Highland factor.

115 R.H. MacDonald, 'Estate of Chisholm, Surviving Rental Lists of 1665 to 1871,' *Transactions of the Gaelic Society of Inverness* LIV (1984-86), pp. 119-28.

XII

Factors in the Clearances

The heaviest, most onerous, work in Highland management was also its most controversial and best known. The role of the Highland estate factor in the Clearances is infamous and we already know a great deal about the critical and dramatic moments of eviction. This was the sharpest point of the restructuring imposed on Highland communities all over the region, though most cataclysmically in the north and north-west. We also know about the great variety of these traumatic moments: most often as individual evictions of single families, usually unheralded and unreported too. At the other extreme were the mass evictions: hundreds of people on notices to quit, physically ousted when they failed to remove, sometimes dragging their feet and, in many instances, mounting degrees of resistance in one form or another.

The great Clearances are generally well-documented and now seared on the popular memory – for instance, those executed by Patrick Sellar, James Gillanders and their kind. They sometimes cleared people on their own behalf (for instance, Sellar and Evander MacIver in Scourie combined factoring with sheep farming and they cleared people off their own farms). Behind them were larger decision makers, notably law firms in perhaps Dingwall or Edinburgh, sometimes acting on behalf of creditors of estates close to bankruptcy. The largest estates operated a hierarchy of management headed by a 'Commissioner' who orchestrated the central policy operations of massive managerial organisations (the most notable was James Loch of the Sutherland Estate from 1812 to 1855, followed by his own son, George, through to 1879). And finally there was the landowner at whose behest, and in whose essential interest, all the policies of 'Improvement' and Clearance were executed. Dividing up responsibility between these different layers of action is complicated and invidious, in part because the lines of communication were long and tenuous, partly because the men on the ground were invested with considerable autonomy and personal discretion, and partly because the lairds often hid behind a veil of aristocratic *hauteur*, feigning innocence and ignorance of what was accomplished in their name.[116] And because they were the instruments of structural change it was part of the factors' responsibility to deflect attention and criticism away from their masters. It was obviously a deeply unpleasant position in Highland life.

The later Clearances, in some respects, occurred at the worst of times, when alternative opportunities were diminishing, when the food supplies were insecure, and populations reached their historical maxima. Clearances in these circumstances were unambiguously harsh and

---

116 The sensitivity of landlords to adverse attention in the press and public opinion at large depended on the attitudes of the individual. An early Irish example of a landlord suddenly retreating from evictions under the spotlight of public scrutiny was that of Lord Fitzwilliam on the Coolattin estate in Wicklow in 1830. He interceded and reversed the policy when challenged in Parliament by O'Connell. See Jim Rees, *Surplus People: The Fitzwilliam Clearances, 1847-1856* (Cork: Collins Press, 2000), p. 24.

heart-wrenching, leaving a deep revulsion against the landlords and their factors. Public opinion was now better informed and more sensitive to the plight of the Highlanders. Landlords were often vacillating, unpredictable, and capricious.

The infamous evictions of 1851 on Barra were conducted in the name of Gordon of Cluny. 'Forced eviction' is an abstract term, distancing and sanitising the grim realities: people were manhandled, there was bloodshed; houses were destroyed, leaving folk roofless in the dead of winter. Gordon, a new owner, was not himself involved directly in these violent scenes. It is clear however that his factors were implicated in these episodes; moreover they already possessed a record of harsh behaviour in previous clearances under General McNeill who was regarded as one of the traditional owners. Gordon of Cluny was described as 'an apathetic absentee' who left the factors as 'masters over their own fiefdoms'.[117]

Such scenes were replayed many times and are well known. That they are not repeated here, does not in any sense diminish them: they colour the entire history of the time of the Clearances. In terms of managerial responsibility three points are evident. First, eviction in any circumstance required physical action, people forced out of their homes against their wishes, usually resentful and uncooperative: evictions were commonplace throughout rural and urban Britain in the nineteenth century; those in Ireland and the Highlands were the most sensational because of their scale and the brutal ousting of defenceless people. Second, the estate factors were following instructions from above, from proprietors who themselves were often performing their own

---

117 Newby declares that emigration was a tragic necessity, whoever the owner. Andrew Newby 'Emigration and Clearance from the island of Barra, c.1770-1858', *Transactions of the Gaelic Society of Inverness* LXI (1998-2000), p.131.

twists and gyrations about the consequences, commonly deflecting responsibility onto their underlings. The factors implemented their orders with more or less humanity, depending on circumstances, time of year, the imperatives of their orders, and their own personalities. In the case of Sellar, for example, his own personality, his own philosophy, and his own impatience were part of the explosive context of the events of 1814 in Strathnaver which led to his trial for culpable homicide two years later. Third, it is evident that repeated delays and bankruptcies, and new owners, eventually created a climax of conflict and strongarmed eviction which a more gradual series of changes might have averted. The trouble was that the introduction of sheep farming was an indivisible process: it was all or nothing, a zero sum process in large degree.

The apparatus of eviction employed a long chain of command and execution. There was a cast of sub factors, local agents, police, legal people, sheriff officers, enforcers, militia – an entire hierarchy of evicting teams. And the factors were sometimes also responsible for resettling the people – not only of getting them out of their old homes but relocating them locally or at some distance. And inevitably there were gaps and agonising time delays in this great shifting of people. Often the new re-settlement plots were not readied or even marked out, the new houses unbuilt. It was often a complete mess – even in the best planned versions. All this was part of the factor's responsibility.

This, taken with the usually sullen, resentful and resistant condition of the people about to be removed, was a perfect recipe for conflict and hatred. The factors faced its full fury. Tempers were frayed, sometimes people on both sides bloodied.

A single instance captures much of the turmoil and danger of an eviction. In March 1820 at Culrain, in the middle of a disturbed district in the south-east of Sutherland bordering on Ross, a dense mass of small tenantry waited for an eviction party organised on behalf of the proprietor, Munro of Novar. Radical resistance to neighbouring Clearances had already been witnessed. At Culrain a sporting tenant had encouraged many small tenants (some of them previously cleared from adjacent estates) to settle on his leased land. Abruptly he terminated his lease and the landowner sought a new tenant, securing a new sheep farmer who insisted on a fully cleared possession of the land. Consequently notices were served on the subtenants and the clearing party was then physically resisted. One report described an episode which was repeated on several occasions: the factor had engaged a body of constables and militia to travel fourteen miles from Tain to Culrain where they 'were opposed by an infuriated Mob of Women, with about 40 or 50 Men amongst them, and on a height a few hundred yards behind them there appeared to be about 200 men drawn up, and many if not the whole of them armed with muskets ...' The removal party was then assailed from behind a stone dyke by the women who 'with most horrible yells and screams, plied us with showers of stones, [by] which many of the persons who came with us were much hurt ... I saw that if I had directed the small party of Militia to fire on them, that the consequence would have been extremely fatal, probably to us all, as if any of their advanced party fell, the men they have in reserve armed could have surrounded and overpowered us.' The sheriff and the factor's party sensibly decided to withdraw in much disarray; had they been caught they would have been humiliated – that is, their summonses of removal seized and burned, and themselves 'stripped naked and thrown in the river.'[118]

---

118 Highland Archives, Inverness, Munro of Novar Papers, D538, letters of MacLeod of Geannies to Lord Advocate from Tain, March 1820.

In this case the fear among the estate and local law officers was the impending loss of all control by legal means in the district. The proprietor, Munro of Novar, was away in London, making efforts to find refuge for the people he was attempting to evict: he had in mind their assisted emigration to the Cape of Good Hope, or, even more improbably, to a re-settlement on Dartmoor. Neither plan was credible, though both plans demonstrated the hopeless naivety of the owner. Eventually, under threat of overwhelming military intervention, the resistance was terminated and the people given more time to leave. This episode, common enough in the long history of the Clearances, demonstrated the opposition of the people, their inability to prevail against authority, and the profoundly unsavoury and unwanted position of the factor in such circumstances.[119]

As another factor in Sutherland remarked of an attempt to re-organise the small tenantry in Assynt in 1848: it was 'a very disagreeable duty to perform – and that it is utterly impossible to get through with it and be popular ... I never took any pains to be make myself popular and never will. I do what I believe to be my duty strictly and impartially and I am certain to gain more respect in this way than any other course.'[120]

Factors often had divided loyalties: pressure from above to raise rents, and from below to keep the people contented. They also had conflicts of interest – some could sense opportunities to benefit from the great changes and stick in their own oars. Factors often took up farms on their own account, not always to the liking of their masters. This happened even before the advent of sheep farming. When the Duke of Argyll in the 1770s received a request from his factor

119 See Eric Richards, *A History of the Highland Clearances* vol. 2 (London: Croom Helm, 1985), p. 312, ff.

120 MacIver to Loch, 7 Jan 1848, Stafford CRO, D593/K/1/3/36

seeking a farm for himself, Argyll was roused to anger: 'I sent you to Tyree to be my factor, to look after and provide interests, and the good of the people, not to be great farmer seeking suddenly to enrich and aggrandise yourself'. In the following century, as James Hunter points out, the factors in general came from the same strata as the sheep farmers, and some of them farmed on their own account, often on favourable terms from the landlord. He points out that some clergy of the Established Church doubled as factors and were complicit in the evictions.[121]

Others, as we have seen, were sacked when they failed to execute the strict and rigorous orders of their masters. Some resigned and left the management; some broke down, fell into financial confusion, became alcoholic, lost their balance.[122] Those who persisted became increasingly professional and authoritarian, fulfilling their duties, even to point of exceeding their orders with an excess of zeal and moral superiority. Andrew Scott on the Cromartie Estate, responsible for mid-century removals which were successfully resisted by the crofters, repeatedly complained that he was in physical danger. He regarded the small tenants as wretched, backward and ignorant, a people full of cunning and deceit and with no understanding of English: they were, he said, 'exceedingly unruly and difficult to manage'.[123]

The range of behaviour, the psychology and the attitudes of the cadre of factors had widened and hardened over the phases of the Clearances. The Highland factor had been required to execute the restructuring of Highland society and to cope with the massive problems generated by unprecedented economic change and population growth. It was a

---

121 Hunter, *Crofting Community*, pp. 39, 120, 144.

122 See, Tindley, 'They sow …', pp. 76-77.

123 Eric Richards and Monica Clough, *Cromartie: Highland Life, 1650-1914* (Aberdeen: Aberdeen University Press, 1989), p. 327.

time of prolonged crisis in the Highlands and the factors were at its centre. Having managed these tumultuous changes, they then found themselves faced with the consequences, including poverty, congestion, and despair, and further shifts in the foundations of Highland life. Invested with immense local authority and responsibility, the Highland factor was often the tool of repression and arbitrary action. They were also deeply conflicted individuals, often driven into extreme frustration and ill health. Understanding the essential contradictions in their roles goes some way to explaining their dark reputations.

XIII

Factoring in the Aftermath

In the aftermath of the Clearances the Highland estate factors faced the consequences of the preceding changes. Many of them, by mid-century, were of a new generation; when they appeared before the Napier Commission in the 1880s (on behalf of their masters) they mostly denied any direct knowledge of the earlier events: they distanced themselves from the events of the Clearances, which were now deeply embedded in the Highland psyche.

Even so, occasional evictions continued in several places; but the context had changed and the public mood was increasingly and effectively opposed to such landlordly behaviour. Nevertheless the factor remained the central figure of authority, especially in the crofter communities. As early the 1770s Dr Johnson had already diagnosed the social malaise that would follow the changes that he had witnessed: 'If the tacksmen be banished, who will be left to impart knowledge or impress civility?' The burden eventually fell on the church ministers as social leaders and there was a polarisation of society. James Loch was keenly conscious of the problem and suggested, improbably, that the sheep farmers step into the role. As Cregeen says, 'The new masters were the factors, often representing a non-resident land owner and usually disliked'. It had become a divided society which had lost its native leaders in a 'polarised landscape.'[124] Meanwhile the average size of the Highland estate had increased greatly.[125]

James Loch had orchestrated the great removals in Sutherland in the period 1816-1821 and knew more than most about the problems of managing change in the Highlands. Twenty years later, now in somewhat mellowed mode, Loch gave advice to the young Marquis of Lorne – advice which captured the changed atmosphere of relations which factors and their masters recognised in the mid-century. Loch explained: 'do nothing too fast or you will fail in gaining your end, for if the people don't go along with you, they will resist in a thousand ways, besides all mankind must be allowed to a certain extent to be happy in their own way.'[126] Factors were expected to be paragons: thus George Loch in 1859 specified the requirements of a new factor for the Tongue factorship: 'the sort of person to be desired is one already having some experience of business, and yet retaining his powers of personal activity and exertion – farming knowledge is not essential, though it would be

---

124 E.A. Cregeen, Recollections, p. 260.

125 Some of the functions of the mid-century Highland estate factor are exemplified in detail in John Munro Mackenzie, Diary 1851, and Richards and Clough, Cromartie, chapter 24 and Appendix ('A month in the life of a Factor: August 1882'). The Lewis factors presided over a territory of 400,000 acres, with a population of almost 20,000 who were dispersed over 100 villages, mainly along the coasts. The factors had great discretionary authority and great responsibilities. At one extreme they were required to extract full rental income from the estate; at the other they were instructed to ensure the people of the estate did not starve to death. They were also expected to readjust the population levels to equate with the carrying capacity of the estate. Munro Mackenzie was a predecessor of Donald Munro of ill fame.

126 Loch to Lorne, 10 July 1846, Sutherland Collection, Stafford County Record Office.

useful – a quiet, calm judgment, firmness, and yet a conciliatory manner.'[127]

Rather despairingly, in June 1880, the Cromartie factor, Gunn, told Loch's successor, Sir Arnold Kemball, that 'It is no easy task to keep order among large numbers of lotters, and there is no part of a Factor's duty which makes more frequent demands upon his tact and judgement.'[128]

The Highlands had by now long readjusted to the cleared landscape and to the residue of a congested and swollen crofting population which declined in numbers only very slowly over the coming decades. In essence the post-clearance Highlands was split between the great sheep farms and the crofting populations. The former were easy to manage – a few very large tenants who paid by far the lion's share of the rental income of the estates. The sheep farmers were mainly concerned with rents and prices, wool yields and market conditions, the status of their leases, and the problem of keeping people and deer off their farms. The sporting tenants by the 1840s had their own very particular demands, but they too were few in number.

There was an explicit recognition at this time that the factor's responsibilities had lessened because many of their duties had diminished. On the great Sutherland estate the Commissioner pointed out that:

> in the earlier days of [the] Factorship, when the measures [ie the removals] were going on, or had been just concluded, for the resettlement of the people in the country, while roads were yet making to open up the country, the while everything was in the process of change. Things had been more onerous then – now it is time to reduce the scale of factoring.[129]

---

127 Loch to Scott, 15 Feb 1859, Cromartie Papers, National Library of Scotland.

128 Gunn to McLellan, 4 Aug 1883, Cromartie Papers, NLS.

129 Loch to Peacock, 1 Nov. 1864, Sutherland Collection, Stafford CRO.

But this seriously understated the problems of managing the remaining populations of crofters.

By the late nineteenth century the factors were often men of substance on large salaries: salaries on the Sutherland estate districts were ranging between £639 and £350 p.a.[130] Morvern had passed through the classic phases of the Highland transformation, including clearances, and by 1851 supported a much diminished population, the result of earlier removals. The new owners, often industrialists from England and the Lowlands, with external sources of wealth, now occupied the estates. Thus Octavius Smith was able and willing to cross-subsidise his estate as a retreat, a pleasure ground for fishing and shooting, perfect for distinguished guests from the south. Patrick Sellar, successful as a great sheep farmer in Sutherland, had bought the nearby Ardtornish estate in 1838 and had set up in considerable style in his own country house.

Highland factors were commonly leaders of social activities, JPs, members of the School Board, and chairmen of the Parochial Board. They wielded immense local power, often exercised with paternalistic care and generosity, but they were not usually answerable for their conduct. They presided over the post-clearance landscape with scant knowledge of the recent past, dealing out occasional benevolence to the much reduced, proletarianised population of the estates, advancing the philosophy of the owners and easing the plight of the poor. They were also made busy with building programmes, and managing the precarious finances of the local economy which had become the victim of world prices, reduced wool prices in particular. They were managers oblivious of the past, simply monitoring the now reduced local society. They were expected to maintain respect

130 Loch to Sutherland 10 Aug 1877, Sutherland Collection, Stafford CRO.

and peace for the owners, also rationalising the crofting system, even towards its extinction.

The factors of Morvern included David Corson, a thirty-six-year-old from Dumfries-shire, appointed in 1850 as 'manager' in place of Peter MacNab, whom Octavius Smith had inherited when he bought the Achranich Estate in 1845. MacNab had possessed only shaky spelling and uncertain book-keeping skills.[131] The local population had already been whittled down from 150 in 1815 to 67 in 1851, and the old communal system had been entirely removed – now they were mainly labourers with only three crofters. The estate was small and unprofitable but Smith, a successful industrialist, while minimising the losses, was evidently prepared to accept the idea of subsidising the estate which was clearly meant to be a retreat and a place of pleasure. Nevertheless Corson was expected to institute improvements and to master *Agricultural Chemistry for Young Farmers* (1843), and to prepare a new building programme. Smith explicitly prohibited any new evictions: he did not want to be regarded as 'one of the depressing procession of Lowland Scots who exploited the Highlands.'[132]

Corson was paid £100 p.a. He was required to do a great deal of travelling – sheep sales in Fort William, Mull, and Strontian, and he had to cope in the 1870s with declining wool prices and holding on to stock piles, hoping for better markets. In 1880 Corson, aged sixty-four, retired to Appin after twenty-nine years' service. He was succeeded by Walter Elliot, a twenty-eight-year-old Selkirk man; 'a better class of man' who could spell and had the manners of a gentleman. He had a fine new house and was employed at £400 p.a. – all in the hope that he would rescue the estate finances,

---

131 Philip Gaskell, *Morvern Transformed: A Highland Parish in the Nineteenth Century* (Cambridge: Cambridge University Press, 1968), p.59.

132 Ibid., p.70

but in reality they were 'past mending'. Moreover not much employment was created by the estate, though the Smiths were regarded as benevolent lairds.

Walter Elliot became a man of substance by the 1890s and he 'controlled the employment of all who worked for the estate, and thereby the living and welfare of over half of the total population of the parish.' He held immense local power, was not answerable for his conduct, and exercised his local authority with paternalistic care and generosity. He appeared before the Napier Commission, but his memory, according to Philip Gaskell, was not accurate.[133]

The role of the factor had been observed by Robert Somers on his tour of the Highlands in 1846. On the Strathspey estate of Sir James Grant all improvements by the tenantry required explicit approval from above: 'a written authority from the factor on the Strathspey to improve, is about as difficult to obtain as a ticket of admission to the present chamber of the Grand Turk'. But Somers declared that the typical factor was a geological fossil – a respectable old tradesman of the old school, often with a hopeless attitude to investment, totally opposed to modern methods – a heavy drag on the wheels of improvements. This was a nice reverse model: Somers, no friend of the landlords, said that the factors should be the missionaries of agricultural improvement and that 'In no department is the incapacity of the Highland lairds more conspicuous'.[134]

In the north and north-west of the Highlands the main task of the factor was the administration of the crofter and cottar populations. Congested, poor and recurrently famished, in many places they constituted a teeming mass of small tenants who were a managerial quandary. In some

---

133 Ibid., p.114.

134 Robert Somers, *Letters from the Highlands on the Famine of 1846,* first published in 1848 (Inverness: Melven, 1985), p. 94.

parts the population was larger than it ever was before, trapped in a declining economy in which fishing and kelping were dying and in which the potato crop was subject to repeated failure. The population of Lewis trebled between 1801 and 1901.[135] The sheer problem of welfare was omnipresent. And there was rising opposition and radicalism among the crofters, often egged on by the ministers. There was no middling group to provide ballast to this society. The polarisation was complete and the crofters tended to blame their continuing poverty on 'the doings of the factors'.[136] Yet the factor was often called upon to settle any difference among the people, which seldom went to any lawsuit.[137]

The Napier Commission into conditions among the crofting population exposed the emotional conflicts of the 1880s. The man who helped to precipitate the Commission (and who also wrote a remarkable *History of the Highland Clearances*) was Alexander Mackenzie. He was born in the late 1830s and had been brought up in Gairloch; he was able to recollect the days of the famine and the work of Dr John Mackenzie who had been the Gairloch factor at the time. Though he subsequently retracted some of his allegations, Alexander Mackenzie painted a devastating picture of factorial oppression associated with an estate which had devoted great efforts to improving the lot of the crofters. Alexander Mackenzie recalled the story of the rejoicing among the crofters at the death of the factor Macleod of Gesto, 'a perfect terror to the people', who died suddenly in 1850-51 and whose memory was execrated in

135 MacDonald, *Lewis*, p. 45.

136 Evidence to the *Napier Commission* quoted by Newby, 'Emigration and clearance,' p. 131. The opposition of interest was given expression by Andrew Scott in the 1841 Report; see Hunter, *Making of the Crofting Community*, p. 82.

137 *New Statistical Account of Scotland*, Gairloch, p. 96.

Gaelic verse. Rigid rules had been applied during 'the disastrous period of the Doctor's factorial rules', which were 'imperiously enforced' and, during the famine, virtually ruined the tenantry 'by taking away their cattle and glutting the market.'

Mackenzie reported that situation in the 1880s, notably the role of 'the local manager, whom the people fear, as they do in most places, much more than a proprietor.' He said 'he would make the people eat one another' before he had done with them. The people were kept in a state of near terror by the factors and especially the ground officers – afraid to open their mouths. 'All the factors and managers of my time have had the "fat of the land" and left the people in poverty.' The game laws were especially draconian: so far as game, rabbits and hares were concerned, 'All a factor has to do is to lift a finger in a township and all the people will not touch an animal.'[138] At the Napier Commission a massive accumulation of crofter grievance was ventilated, and the lion's share was directed at the factors, past and present.

The factors themselves were shocked and horrified at the testimonies of their crofters before the Commission. The indignation of Gunn, factor on the Cromartie estate, was unbounded: 'Oh! Such heartless ingratitude – I cannot get over it ... Such ingratitude it had not been my lot to meet before ... I am bitterly disappointed that they should have been unjust and unfair as well as ungrateful ... out of a population of over 1000 there was not one who had the moral courage to speak one word of acknowledgment of anything that had ever been done by their noble and kind

---

138 Dr John Mackenzie was a factor in the old mould – that is, a younger relative who was brought into the estate management. He himself was a farmer in Easter Ross. Alexander Mackenzie reported that the ground officers were especially malevolent, thereby pushing responsibility further down the chain of authority: see *Napier*, q. 41083.

proprietors.'[139] Gunn's reaction was typical of the tremendous expression of factorial bitterness at the time of the Napier Commission. The morale, and indeed the authority, of the factors had been profoundly undermined.

This soon became the new context in which the factors were responsible for the maintenance of the fragile estate order. Moreover the social psychology of factoring had shifted. In the early phases of the Clearances there had been an understanding that many landlords were attempting to renovate and replace the old system, to introduce new industries and infrastructures for the benefit of all. Such optimism had long since departed and now the prevailing managerial philosophy was that of reducing the population and eventually amalgamating the crofts into larger farms – in effect, to disperse and reduce the population and dismantle the crofting system. This of course was resisted tooth and nail by the crofting population which had clung on with extraordinary resilience and fortitude, not to mention a measure of bloody-mindedness. There was barely even a minimum of cooperation.

By the 1870s many of the factors were managing a crofting system in which they had no belief, no intellectual commitment. By this time the depleted social structure gave little social cohesion, and the authority of the factors was widely subverted by ministers and radicals. Most of all, they were required to manage the congested crofter and cottar populations. It was an impossible task, punctuated by the needs of famine relief and the effort to induce emigration.[140] They perceived the only solution to the remaining Highland

---

139 NLS, Cromartie Papers, Gunn to Kemball, 22 June 1880.

140 The role of factors in the destitution of 1837 is touched upon by John MacAskill in his Introduction to *The Highland Destitution of 1837: Government Aid and Public Subscription* (Edinburgh: Scottish History Society, 2013), pp. xxxv-xxxvii. See also Tindley, 'They Sow ...', p. 72.

problem to be the reduction of the population by selective dispersion and the enlargement of holdings. Often they were managing a mutinous and sullen population which, by the 1870s, had become actively rebellious and literally ungovernable.

The new generation of factors had inherited a broken-backed structure which now became a managerial nightmare, and often they were the scapegoats. They were running a system for which they had no intellectual conviction and only minor sympathy.[141] They simply did not believe that crofting was a going concern, nor a viable system.[142] The Napier Commission, of course, had exposed the depth of feeling in which they were deluged.[143] The factors disclaimed all knowledge of, or responsibility for, the previous changes, most notably for the Clearances. They had closed their minds to the past. Crofting came to be regarded as an absurd survival which penalised all parties and future generations. The crofters mainly took the opposite view – that this was their life and their preference, their inherited right. There was therefore a diametrical opposition of outlook and philosophy. To the factors, and many of their masters, crofting was an anachronism and a problem to manage and

141 Cf., Tindley, 'They Sow …', p. 71.

142 As Cregeen puts it, 'The crofter's economy in the 19th century was in contrast with the big farmers, almost as much a subsistence economy as that of the small tenants in the 17th century. They could pay their rents to the factor with a beast and relied on a pig for most of their meat supplies'. The crofter survived 'by his very lack of need and his inability to accommodate to the climate and the environment.' They seemed hopelessly out of tune with the times. Remnants of communality remained as a perfect anachronism. Cregeen, *Recollections*, pp. 260-61.

143 In the Napier Report it was asserted that much of the evidence presented was of doubtful validity and specifically that 'Many of the allegations of oppression and suffering with which these pages are painfully loaded would not bear a searching examination'. Quoted by a hostile critic, Joseph Shield Nicholson, *Examination of the Crofters' Commission Report* (Edinburgh, 1884), p.8.

preferably to diminish. This of course added to the tensions; it was a recipe for conflict and endless squabbling and became a constant headache for them. Their only conviction was to rationalise crofting, to terminate the old system altogether. But the people were determined to survive and to prevail.[144]

The profession of factoring itself had no corporate sense, no uniformity, no institution to represent the factors: some of them acted as brakes on further change; others were ruthless, and some broke down in body and soul under the strain.[145] When Valentine Smith died in 1906 he bequeathed £1,000 to his factor Elliot who died a few weeks later. But factors were vulnerable, easily seduced by the temptations of their position. Others fell into financial difficulties of their own making, even the most upright of them. Thus Andrew Scott from Hawick had been a farmer who went bankrupt in 1830 before he became factor on the Cromartie Estate: he was still embarrassed by his outstanding debts in 1851 when he faced personal danger among the riotous population of Coigach. When George Gunn, the factor of the Sutherland estate, died his financial affairs were in spectacular disorder. He was found to be £20,000 in debt and his affairs 'an awful smash'. This calamity exposed evidence of malpractice: Gunn had evidently channelled estate rents into his own account. Nevertheless the estate wiped the slate clean and looked after his widow.[146] Gunn had borrowed £4,000 from his fellow factor, Evander MacIver, who was also damaged in the scandal.

---

144 The problem of discipline is covered in Tindley, 'They Sow ...', p. 73.

145 Annie Tindley emphasises the stress and strain on factors and the breakdown in health of some of them in the late nineteenth century, partly attributable to psychological tensions, especially at the time of the Napier Commission. The post-Commission regimes added greatly to the strain they felt by increasing factorial workloads. See Annie Tindley, 'They Sow ...', pp. 71, 78, 74.

146 Ibid., p.78.

MacIver himself had arrived in Sutherland in 1844: in effect he inherited the post-clearance conditions. A Gaelic-speaking Lewisman, he had a remarkable career in Scourie which lasted for half a century, during which time he totally dominated his district and left a severe reputation. However, early in this career, in 1861, MacIver fell into his own financial crisis: according to George Loch, the estate Commissioner, MacIver had become a 'hopeless embarrassment'. Loch described him as 'stupid and dishonest' and he was very close to being sacked. Despite the intense embarrassment Loch kept MacIver on in the Scourie management for another thirty years.

MacIver's main task was that of managing the crofters of Scourie and this turned into outright turmoil in the 1870s. They were becoming increasingly mutinous and independent and, in common with estate managers across the Highlands, MacIver faced the crofters' movement which had gained such momentum: by the early 1880s they could no longer maintain or manage the post-clearance inheritance.

The idea of restoring land to the crofters, or giving them more land, was totally anathema to MacIver. His situation was filled with philosophical tensions whereby he found himself administering a system in which he had no conviction.[147] Yet it was also a system which was running out of control, challenging his capacity to maintain its order and expectations. This was the cause of his intense personal frustration, which expressed itself in his dealings with both the tenantry and his employers. In these years he witnessed, almost helplessly, the reinstatement and preservation of the crofting system, which he regarded as absurd and unworkable. For a believer in the inevitable march of rational progress,

---

147 Cf. Annie Tindley and Eric Richards, 'Turmoil among the crofters: Evander McIver and the Highland question, 1873-1903', *Agricultural History Review* 60 (2012), pp. 191-213; and Tindley 'They Sow ...', p. 75.

the maintenance and, after 1886, the protection of the crofting system was a disaster. Napier changed the context of factoring and reduced many of the traditional powers of the factor, making their job still more difficult.[148] Many of them, not least MacIver, writhed in frustration at their new impotence.

Ultimately, despite the drama of the warring times, the core of the 'crofting problem' remained. MacIver had conceded that he had not been able to rationalise or reduce the crofting population.

---

148 See Tindley and Richards, 'Turmoil among the Crofters.'

XIV

Cracking under Strain

The 'Improvers' of the late eighteenth century had believed
that they could restructure the Highlands to achieve the joint
result of an efficient commercial agriculture together with an
expanded population on the new foundation of industry and
a new agriculture. In the end it was a failure and the final
result was a deeply unsatisfactory compromise: the remnant
of the population survived while great tracts of land were
used for not very remunerative returns with sheep and deer.

In reality, the crofters had resisted the changes sought
by the estates and the factors; indeed, despite their poverty
and isolation, they had persisted into the twentieth century
and beyond, clinging on against all odds.[149] It was, in some
ways a triumph of their spirit or, less progressively, a triumph
of inertia. The old equilibrium survived, despite the factors,
despite poverty.

It is not difficult to view the factors' position as packed
with tension and contradiction, and greater than elsewhere,

---

149 Annie Tindley, *The Sutherland Estate 1850-1920: Aristocratic Decline,
Estate Management and Land Reform* (Edinburgh: Edinburgh University
Press, 2010), p. 21.

and perhaps more complicated than their counterparts' position, even in Ireland. The fiction of social tradition was more strained in the Highlands. It was a prolonged and bitter contest between the crofters and the management – this is indeed explicit in the evidence of MacIver before the Napier Commission. Few landlords represented themselves before the Commission: their factors were the instruments of a deeply unpopular policy, and they had inherited a broken-backed system. They were invested with a great deal of discretionary authority and free from the direct supervision of their masters.

The factors were, therefore, the products of a system of extreme land monopoly and regional retrogression. They were also the products of a culture in which there was no consultation with the people over whom they exerted so much local authority. It was a system that began to crack in the 1870s when the existing established order at last faced the full consequences of the adverse circumstances of which the factors were both makers and victims.

....

Eric Richards is Emeritus Professor of History at Flinders University, Adelaide, Australia. He was born in Wales, studied at Nottingham University and moved to Australia in the 1960s. He has written several books, including an acclaimed biography of Patrick Sellar, which was awarded the prize for Scottish History Book of the Year by the Saltire Society in 1999. In 2014 he accepted the post of Carnegie Trust Centenary Professor at the University of the Highlands and Islands.